THE SUPERVISOR AS AN INSTRUCTOR
A Guide for Classroom Training

FOURTH EDITION

MARTIN M. BROADWELL
Training Consultant

ADDISON-WESLEY PUBLISHING COMPANY, INC.
Reading, Massachusetts • Menlo Park, California • New York
Don Mills, Ontario • Wokingham, England • Amsterdam
Bonn • Sydney • Singapore • Tokyo • Madrid • San Juan

Library of Congress Cataloging in Publication Data

Broadwell, Martin M.
    The supervisor as an instructor.

    Includes index.
    1. Teaching.   2. School supervisors.   I.   Title.
LB1025.2.B738   1984   371.1'02   83-22297
ISBN 0-201-10356-7

The publisher offers discounts on this book when ordered in quantity for special sales. For more information please contact:
    Corporate & Professional Publishing Group
    Addison-Wesley Publishing Company
    Route 128
    Reading, Massachusetts 01867

ISBN 0-201-10356-7
HIJ-DO-89

Ninth Printing, July 1990

To the women in my life:
My Mother
My Wife
My Daughter

ACKNOWLEDGMENTS

Few jobs which are completed—whether good or bad—are completed without the help of other people who usually contribute more than they receive credit for. This book is no exception. Acknowledgment is made to the following friends in appropriate categories:

Bosses who let me experiment . . .
Bill Sullivan
Zeb Burnett

Trainers who kept me honest . . .
Bob Mager
Dugan Laird

People who thought I knew what I was doing . . .
Cabot Jaffee
Johnny Sajem (who also supplied some of the artwork)
Norm Stanton

Person who defies categorization . . .
R. Peter Rigg

The author also wishes to express appreciation to Resources for Education and Management, Inc., for permission to use some of the artwork from a series of filmstrips on "The Supervisor as an Instructor" and to Lois Winston, who updated several of these art pieces.

PREFACE TO THE FOURTH EDITION

Can it be that over five years have gone by since the revision of the Third Edition? What's happened since then to warrant another edition? Actually, several things have happened that make it again necessary to put more words down and delete others. First, as will always be the case, the technology changes. We're doing some things better now than we were five years ago, we're doing things differently and maybe better, we're not doing some things we thought were good ideas five years ago. Each of these factors suggests a need for another revision.

But there's something else. Few authors are ever happy with the way things were said—after a few months or years have gone by. Having used the book in many classes, this author is fed up with certain words, or phrases, or suggestions which, while not wrong, just don't say it quite the way it should be said. At the time, there is that mental note, "If I ever revise this thing, I want to change that!" If, when the rewriting starts, memory serves well, those things are remembered and changed. There is some of that in this revision.

There are significant changes in six of the chapters and an additional chapter has been added. In Chapter 1, more emphasis is placed on the uniqueness of the adult learner, and a checklist for the *Characteristics of a Good Instructor* is included—something that's been needed for a long time, though this list is certainly not exhaustive. In Chapter 6 *Job Descriptions and Job Standards* are dealt with in more detail, making it easier to understand how to write *Objectives* in the next chapter. Chapter 10 points out the importance of getting *involvement* and *feedback;* now it has some specific examples and cases so that the teacher will find it easier to use these teaching tools. There is a list of ways to induce involvement, and a further discussion on what to do with the feedback that results from the involvement. Some rules for *Preparing Visual Aids* are given in Chapter 11. Even though instructors don't always prepare their own, they should know some of the rules so that they can give intelligent suggestions to those who do the preparation.

Chapter 14 has always dealt with Classroom Techniques. This edition expands it to add current information on *Computer Assisted Instruction* and *Interactive Video.* These subjects are not discussed fully, but trainers are provided with enough information to get a feel for what these techniques are intended to do, and where their strengths and weaknesses are. (No doubt the Fifth Edition—whenever it is published—will expand considerably on these techniques.)

Chapter 18 has been revised to give even more substance to the matter of *Evaluation of Training.* The most significant thing in the addition is a checklist of some length that's intended to create further awareness that many things besides what the instructor does during the training sessions affect its outcome. The checklist shows that there are things that happen before the trainees come in, while they are there, and even when they get back to the job, that control retention, application, and commitment to the skills produced in the classroom.

The most extensive addition is a new chapter, Chapter 19, entitled "Handling the Problem Students." This has been the most frequently requested addition, and the thing that instructors—experienced and new—have the greatest concern about at one time or another. Throughout the book, even in the First Edition, there were suggestions on how to handle problems that arise in the classroom with students, but this chapter brings all of these together, and adds other kinds of problems. The answers may not be perfect, but at least every solution offered is working for someone in circumstances similar to those described in the chapter.

Finally, let's make a pact between you the reader and me the author: teaching people to do something they can't do ought to be rewarding and fun. Writing about how to be a good teacher ought to be equally fun and rewarding. These things being true, let's agree that at such time that the fun and reward cease to be there, we'll both get out of the business!

Decatur, Georgia   M.M.B.
December 1983

PREFACE TO THE THIRD EDITION

It is frightening to think that this book was last revised in 1970. In the rapidly changing world of training, that's somewhere around the Middle Ages. It was first revised after two years, and some major additions, as well as changes, were made then. It is perhaps indicative of the "state of the art" in the training world that this third edition does not have many changes; it has mostly *additions*. This can be interpreted as meaning that what we know now is relatively safe but we're adding to our body of knowledge, rather than finding out we're wrong on many counts. This isn't to say that we aren't wrong: it just means that nobody has found it out yet!

There are important additions in seven of the chapters. Perhaps the most significant additions of all are the ones that give some "systems" of instruction and techniques of teaching. These are in Chapter 14. There are three systems discussed that will include most forms of instructing. There is also a lengthy addition in that chapter on specific techniques, giving a description of each technique and showing the advantages and disadvantages of each.

There are numerous additions that are short but significant. For example, in Chapter 18 there is a brief but important addition on the subject of *evaluation*. The concept that the measure of good training is done ultimately back on the job by looking at operating results is essential to fully understanding our efforts at measuring our training. Chapter 8 has an important addition in a short explanation of the concept of "positive reinforcement."

In addition to the changes mentioned above, we have tried to

update the book with meaningful discussion of more recent evo-
lutions in training, such as video, open classroom, and self-directed learning. It is hoped that all of this will add to the
teaching/learning influence of this book, which is still called a
"guide," not a "rule."

Decatur, Georgia   M.M.B.
November 1977

PREFACE TO THE SECOND EDITION

Several items have been added to make this edition a better tool for the job of training supervisors to be good instructors.

"Task Analysis"—that essential ingredient for a successful training program—has been given an entire chapter. Not only is there a discussion of *what* task analysis is and *why* it is needed, but there is help on *how* to do a good job of analyzing the task for which training is being provided.

"Evaluation of Training" is a subject that is talked about a great deal but pursued only halfheartedly by many people. Chapter 18 gives some suggestions on how to accomplish the job of evaluating the degree of success obtained in improving the performance back on the job.

The most noticeable change is the addition—at the end of each chapter—of exercises and questions. These are provided to allow for participation and involvement when the training is carried out by having a group of supervisors study the material together. The exercises also serve as ready *objectives* for the person who reads the book on his own. He should be able to give meaningful answers to the question in light of what he has read. (In general, the exercises and questions are "mind-stretching" in nature, not just something that can be answered by parroting words from the chapter studied.)

I hope that all these additions will make the book what it is intended to be: a practical handbook for guiding supervisors toward being better *producers of learning*.

Decatur, Georgia   M.M.B.
November 1969

PREFACE TO THE FIRST EDITION

Not all instruction is good instruction. Self-evident as this statement may seem, industrial training in general has failed to recognize the truth of it. Since training time is valuable time in terms of the bottom line, the instructor must be made aware of his responsibility for seeing that his class members take away with them as much as possible of what he has to give. He cannot assume, just because he *told them* something, that they now *have it,* and he cannot assume that they are now able to do something better than they could before they came to class. He cannot simply *assume* that he has taught them well.

There is no stereotype of a good instructor. Certainly it is not enough just to know the subject, essential though that knowledge is. Some things a prospective instructor can learn will help his students retain more of what they are supposed to, but perhaps the single most important quality of a good instructor (other than thorough knowledge of his material) is a willingness to accept the responsibility for the *learning* that should take place as a result of his teaching effort. Once he develops a concern for what those he teaches will be able to do on their jobs, he will find it easier to develop teaching techniques.

It is the purpose of this book to:

1. Cause the instructor to develop a concern for the results of his teaching efforts.

2. Provide a practical guide which will enable the instructor to develop his own teaching techniques.

3. Answer the questions most often asked by the prospective, untrained instructor.

4. Provide specific examples and tests by which the industrial instructor can measure his efforts.

5. Create in the instructor an awareness of the problems industrial students bring to the classroom, and enable him to cope with these problems in the learning situation.

Decatur, Georgia   M.M.B.
October 1967

CONTENTS

PROLOGUE

Employees cannot be trained theoretically. It is useless, then, to train instructors with a theoretical approach. Employees learn in a realistic environment; therefore their instructors must be prepared to train them realistically.

This book is based on the experience gained from a number of years of training would-be instructors, telling them what will and will not work, then having to face them after they have tried out what they were taught. This has a tendency to produce a realistic attitude!

The supervisor assigned to train employees grasps quickly, and sometimes desperately, for a practical approach to instructing. This book is designed to provide that approach.

chapter 1
LOOKING AT THE INSTRUCTOR

The supervisor is paid to handle various activities relating to production. One of those activities is the *training of people*, which may be merely a "look-over-their-shoulders-and-show-them" type of training, supervision of on-the-job training, or a formal classroom assignment. For the most part, this book will deal with formal classroom activity. The careful reader will note, however, that much of what is said concerns getting information to the learner, the principles of which apply in almost any learning situation.

Before going further, let's ask ourselves, "Why do we teach?" So far as the supervisor is concerned, the answer is obvious—to enable the worker to do his job properly. You see, there are two major reasons why a person doesn't do a job; either the person is careless, or doesn't know how to do it. If a person is careless, the correction must come from within, although the supervisor can help him or her develop a sense of job pride. But if the person lacks knowledge, the answer is training.

So that is why we train an employee, because he or she doesn't know how to do a particular job. The supervisor does know how, so he or she does the training. Here we have an important criterion: *A person receives training because of a lack of certain knowledge, and the good instructor should know just what knowledge that person lacks.* This may sound trite, but many instructors simply do not know what information their students lack. What's more, many other instructors don't know what their students should be able to do when they leave the class. (A later chapter will deal with the importance of objectives in some detail).

A good instructor is one who can get needed information to

nis or her students. Expand on this all you like; the fact remains that the instructor's job is to get information from whatever source or form it is in to the student who needs it.

WHY DO WE TEACH AS WE DO?

This rather general description of what a good instructor does fails to satisfy our organized minds, because we expect to have a checklist by which to measure our results. To clarify, let's ask ourselves why we teach as we do. That is, why do we use a particular technique (if we have one), or why do we teach in a haphazard manner (if that's what we do)? This is a critical point, by the way, because if we are to argue that one method is better than another, then we are saying it makes a difference how we teach, and *if it makes a difference, then our own way may not be the best.*

THE UNIQUENESS OF TEACHING IN THE HERE AND NOW

One thing that needs to be mentioned about teaching adults, especially those from the work world, is a "short-term" element that is quite different from other educational efforts. Most courses offered in the work world are short in duration—often one or two days and seldom more than two to three weeks. While many of these courses last for six to eight hours a day, the teachers have to learn much about the students very quickly. There isn't time for the luxury of taking a month or six weeks just to "settle in" with the students. The rapport must be established almost from the first hour, and the students must like the environment and accept the instructor and the goals of the course immediately. There can be very little time set aside for adapting to the situation.

It may be that this one factor—the shortness of the course—is as important as any other reason for preparing oneself before teaching the course. The teacher has no time to fumble around or try out things. He or she must have everything ready and from the opening bell must be able to show the students the objectives and how they'll be reached. Good relationships must be established immediately. There can be no time for the teacher to begin to wear well or to learn to get along with the group, and he or she can't have idiosyncrasies that the students must learn to get along with.

How can preparation help? The teacher can plan ahead of time to get the students involved in the learning process instead of engaging in nonlearning "warm-up" exercises. Even the "ice-breakers" should be things that aid in getting to the objectives. In the planning stages the instructor looks for ways of getting the students into the learning process as quickly as possible and plans the first activities accordingly. Rather than using the usual lengthy lectures and introductions, the teacher will perhaps introduce some small-group activities on a topic general enough for all to participate in but specific enough to produce usable learning. This allows the students to become productive during their very first activity in the class, reduces the importance of the instructor's personality, and allows the students to start off understanding that their reason for being there is to learn rather than to like the instructor.

SHOULD WE IMITATE?

Assuming we have not really studied the question, we probably teach the way we do for one of several reasons. The most common reason is that our way seems natural to us. Then again, we may teach as we do because someone we liked (or thought was a good instructor) taught that way. A third reason may be that we have experimented and feel that our way of teaching is the best way. This is a better reason than the first two, and if the experimentation was conducted properly, and still continues, then our method of instruction is probably pretty good.

Let's examine our first reason. If doing what comes naturally produces the desired learning, then it is good technique. If not, it's bad. The trouble with it is that many supervisors find that what comes naturally to them is *talk*. They feel quite relaxed and natural leaning against a sturdy lectern and lecturing away from a voluminous set of notes. But the chances are very good that their class isn't learning much.

What about imitation? Well, it may be the sincerest form of flattery, but it is not necessarily the best way to become a good instructor. Consider a few examples:

There are those that succeed by clever use of humor (note: *clever*). Supervisor A had a successful instructor who told jokes, kidded around, and taught her subject very well. *But here we need to make an important point.* It is quite possible for a trainee to enjoy a class, to look forward to it and feel that it passes quickly, without learning much from it. Supervisor A's instructor had mastered her technique; unless he can do likewise, Supervisor A may fail to teach what his trainees are supposed to learn.

The timing, type, and extent of humor are all important. Not everyone can use it, and those who cannot should leave it alone. But even the instructor who can use humor should not do so to make a reputation as a humorist. Proper use of humor can put the class at ease, provide a transition from one topic to another, and emphasize important points, but it should not be used for its own sake.

Supervisor B once had an instructor who kept the students captivated. This instructor sat on the desk with his legs crossed and wore a black turtleneck sweater. If Supervisor B tried to imitate these mannerisms there is a good chance that he would not be a successful instructor. In the first place, such mannerisms would not be his own, and a good instructor should be himself or herself so far as possible. In the second place, this could be a trap; it may be that the unorthodox instructor was effective in spite of his posture and dress, rather than because of them.

Supervisor C had a college mathematics teacher who reduced everything to simple arithmetic and was very effective as an instructor. So Mr. C decides to imitate. But suppose his class came to him well prepared, with a good background and a desire to get deeper into the subject. Mr. C. will lose his students' attention in a hurry as soon as he reduces a few things "back to arithmetic."

On the other hand, Supervisor D was most impressed by a college professor who challenged the students to dig out the information for themselves. She presented the material once, erased the board before the class could even copy what she had written, then went on to the next point. "We really had to study, but we learned it," says Mrs. D. But did they learn because the professor taught, or did they burn the midnight oil and teach themselves? Did they learn because they had to in order to graduate? Could they have learned more if the professor had used a different method? If Mrs. D chooses to imitate this method and confronts a room full of new, inexperienced employees, she may do them a real disservice, and most likely will fail as an instructor.

So imitation is not a guaranteed road to success. There are times when imitation works, just as humor works. If one instructor's teaching technique is effective and another can use it with equally good results, then it should be copied. But there is no other good reason for imitation.

IS THERE A STEREOTYPE FOR THE INSTRUCTOR?

If imitation is not always in order, are we suggesting that there is no stereotype for a good instructor? Well, there are some things that good instructors have in common, but ask a number of people to list the top five characteristics of a good instructor and most likely none of the lists will contain all the same items. As we shall see later, it is more accurate to say that the *students* of good teachers are stereotyped, than to say that there is a stereotype for good teachers. They are the students who participate, who are involved, who build on existing knowledge, and so on. *But instructors may produce this action in entirely different ways,* one with frequent quizzes, another with oral discussions, yet another by introducing controversy.

If we recognize that learning is a complex procedure, we will understand that instruction is, too. It would be nice to establish a pattern of instructor requirements; we could "plug in" the supervisors who fitted it and remold those who didn't. But for our purposes a theoretical approach to teaching can prove a trap, involving lengthy discussion of various learning theories, without ever settling on a sure way to produce learning. Every effort will be made to keep the contents of this book as practical and realistic as possible, its purpose being to enable supervisors to feel more confident in the classroom and to help them direct their actions, whatever form they take, toward the students' needs.

CHARACTERISTICS OF A GOOD INSTRUCTOR

It is very difficult to list a set of characteristics by which to identify a good teacher. Successful instructors do not have a certain list of things in common—at least not on the surface. Some seem to be good at their jobs by doing one thing, while others seem to be just as good by doing the opposite. However, when we look more closely, we see some things that are common to all the instructors whom we list under the "good" category. Without suggesting that the list is complete, let's look at some of the important ones:

1. *Ability to convince students that he/she wants to help them learn.*
   These instructors don't look alike in the classroom so it's hard to find two who appear the same. They may be very "down-to-earth", easy to talk to, given to using "earthy" type examples, and seemingly without many concerns in the world. Or they may be very formal and very serious, giving the idea that the class is a serious place to be and the students are expected to refrain from foolishness. Whatever demeanor they have, one thing shows through it all: they view the classroom activities as the means by which their students will learn what they came to learn, and that for that to happen the instructor must do everything he or she can to help them.

2. *Enthusiasm for learning.*
   This is a natural consequence of the first characteristic; the easiest way the teacher can convince students he or she wants them to learn is to be enthusiastic about their learning. This doesn't mean that everyone who is an enthusiastic, vibrant person is automatically a great teacher. Vibrancy is a good quality when combined with some other things, but it is not what we're talking about here. Some very enthusiastic and energetic people fail to make it as good instructors because the students find out they're more *pep* than *prep*. These instructors expect their energy and brightness to make up for the time they should have been preparing, studying, and organizing.
   Those successful teachers who are able to get enthusiastic about teaching anything they're qualified to teach deserve much for their effort. They recognize it's easier to teach something that is "fun" to teach. They know that every teacher has some favorite subjects which they prefer to expound on in front of the group. They also recognize

the importance of students going out of a class able to do what the course was designed to teach them to do, and that's what gets them *really* excited. Simply put, successful teachers get their excitement from learners learning the subject rather than from the subject itself.

3. *Ability to organize the information to be taught.*
Not all teachers know their subjects as well as they should, and this obviously makes for a bad teaching-learning situation. But there are also those who know the material and have experience in the field, but who still can't do the job as well as they should. The problem is often the instructor's lack of ability to organize the knowledge mentally in such a way that it will come up at the time and place needed.

This isn't an easy skill to acquire, and it requires some good study habits. It is more than just knowing the material, putting in a lot of study time, and having a lot of experience in the field being talked about. The instructor has to be able to know what he or she knows and doesn't know, and must be able to recall the information at the right time for maximum learning power.

This is best illustrated when a successful instructor is discussing a subject and a student asks a question slightly off the subject, but closely related to the general field. The good instructor has the ability to make a quick mental review of the question and then make a determination as to whether his or her reservoir of usable data has sufficient information immediately available to answer the question. If so, and it seems appropriate to pursue the direction the answer will take, then the question is dealt with. If there isn't enough knowledge there, the question is tabled or dropped with something like, "I'm sorry, but that's something I can't deal with without more study." The quality we're talking about is not only knowing what is known and not known, but also being able to bring up what is known at the time it's needed.

4. *Patience to wait for the learner to learn.*
The new teacher (along with some who have not learned the patience required to let the learners get their own "ah

ha's") is prone to get "itchy" and restless when a student asks a question or doesn't respond immediately to a question from the teacher. Silence is frightening, and the impatient teacher wants to fill in that silence as quickly as possible instead of letting the learner dangle for awhile, doing some thinking and pondering and even getting a little impatient. There is an old saying that goes something like, "Learning starts with a problem and ends with a solution." There is every evidence that it is a true saying! When we ask students a question and they don't have the answer immediately available, they naturally expect the teacher to give them the answer. If the teacher does not, they're a little uncomfortable. The same is true when they ask the teacher a question, they expect an answer. In both cases the successful instructor knows that the student is confronted with a problem. This should be a good time for some learning to take place, BUT it isn't likely to take place if the teacher simply gives the answer and goes into a lengthy discussion on the subject. As soon as the student gets the answer the mind door will likely close, and the ensuing discussion is superfluous.

What does the good instructor do? Exercise patience! He or she knows that the world of learning won't end if the students don't have the answer dished out to them and does a little subtle "baiting" by asking some leading questions which the students can answer with a little thought. Then there is another question and some more thought and . . . finally there is that, "Ah ha! I see now!" from the student.

5. *Working knowledge of the subject.*
There is more to teaching a subject than just knowing something about that subject. In the practical world of the adult workforce, it is important that the students learn things that have to do with their everyday job. This requires both a knowledge of the subject being taught and the ability to apply that knowledge. It is more than just a matter of having a lot of experience, though that certainly helps. It is more than knowing more about the subject than those people working on the job, though that helps

too. It is a matter of being able to take the knowledge of the subject and the knowledge of the job and put the two together in a way that's meaningful to the students.

Teachers who have this ability to bring reality out of knowledge get such statements on their critiques as, "This was something I can use when I get back," "This is new, but I can see the application. I'll be able to do my job much better by using this newly learned technique." "It's sure nice to learn from somebody who's been there and knows that my problems are. . . ." The capable teacher would much rather hear remarks of that kind than those which proclaim how much the instructor knew about the subject. (Perhaps that was best expressed by one student's critique, "The teacher sure did know a lot about this subject . . . unfortunately, when the class was over, he was still the only one who knew anything about it."

6. *Empathy and the ability to get empathy.*
There are those teachers who either from their own past experience or from listening to the students, have developed the ability to know how their students are feeling. They understand what it's like to go 30 minutes past lunch no matter how interesting the subject is. They know what the students are thinking when the teacher is wasting time that has to be made up at the end of the day. They have a feeling for the student who is trying but getting nowhere, or the student who already knows the subject and finds the material boring and elementary. All of this knowledge comes under the characteristic of having "empathy." It is a good quality. Good instructors have it, bad ones don't.

There is another side of the empathy issue. Many good instructors have developed a unique ability to make the students empathetic for them as instructors. It relates to what we said earlier about teachers who can convince students that they want them to learn and will help them as much as possible. When the students understand this, they return empathy that provides understanding when the equipment doesn't work, the material is misprinted, the video is the wrong one, or the teacher makes a blunder on a certain subject. We aren't sure just how teachers get it or get their students to have it, but it's a fine quality and sets many instructors apart from others.

No doubt there are other characteristics, traits, and skills that successful instructors have in common, but these seem to be the most important and the ones most often seen in good teachers. None are really very mysterious or all that difficult to acquire. Fortunately for most teachers, it is possible to teach without all of these. It's just much easier and much better when the instructors have some or all of them in good quantities!

Exercises and Questions

1. Let all persons in the group make their own lists of characteristics of a good instructor. Divide the group into subgroups of three or four persons each and have each subgroup come up with a list of five "essential" characteristics of a good instructor. Compare the lists from the different subgroups and record the common items on the board. From this "master" list, have the entire group pick—by voting—the single most important characteristic. Discuss why there isn't complete agreement on the essential characteristics of a "good instructor."

2. Looking at the list on the board from Question 1, discuss how you would determine whether a person *really* had each characteristic if you had never known the person or seen him or her teach.

3. Let students think of the best instructor they ever had in any teaching situation (school, church, Boy Scouts, on the job, etc.) and make a list of the characteristics that person had that made him or her a good instructor. Was the list comparable to the one on the board?

4. What do we mean when we say that a certain person is a "good" teacher?

chapter 2
THE TEACHING PROCESS

When supervisors first enter the classroom as instructors, they may doubt their ability to handle their new assignment. They should be careful, though, not to let this feeling work against them. In overcoming their fears, they may tend to protect themselves by attempting to memorize a lecture, or by sticking strictly to their extensive notes. They may even work up a good "show," which could produce plaudits but little or no learning.

MEASUREMENT OF INSTRUCTOR QUALITY

This raises the question of how one measures the quality of an instructor. First we need a simple definition of his or her job. We can grasp the task better if we think of the instructor's function as that of getting information from some source to the mind of the trainee. This information exists in a book or a set of instruction manuals or as part of the experience of the supervisor, but the trainee does not have it. The instructor's responsibility is not just to provide the information, but to provide it in usable form, that is, a form that will produce the desired results back on the job.

The tendency, though, is to measure the *classroom performance* of the instructor, rather than the end result, the *learning*. It is easy to observe an instructor's presentation and get the feeling that he or she is doing a superb job. The instructor may exude confidence, have the right answers to all questions and appear to be doing excellent work. To pass judgment at this point, however, is a big mistake. There is only one true measure of an instructor's quality; *are the trainees learning what they are intended to learn*?

HOW GOOD ARE CONVENTIONAL METHODS?

In measuring the quality of instructors we have a tendency to judge them in terms of conventional teaching methods. If they do what others have done before them, and do it well, we may classify them as good teachers. For example, they may deliver smooth, well-prepared lectures. Their notes may be in good order and their delivery beyond reproach. We compare their presentations with those of others who have lectured not quite so well, and we rate them about average. Well, they may be fine *lecturers,* but that does not necessarily mean that they are fine *instructors.*

The typical classroom is much like the typical American; it probably doesn't exist. But it is important for us to consider the layout and contents of most industrial classrooms. In general, they are set up with alternating chairs and tables, perhaps with an aisle down the middle. At the front will be a chalkboard or perhaps some means of writing on paper. A portable or pull-down projection screen will probably be available. Somewhere at the front will be a lectern. It may be a large, solid, floor-length one or a small table model, but a lectern there will be.

There may be other devices, arrangements, and facilities, but the ones described here are typical of what supervisors can expect as they begin their teaching assignments. These are their tools. *It is their skill in using them that will determine their success as instructors.*

The conventional way to approach a classroom situation (after preplanning) is to enter and begin covering the material. The lectern becomes the center of attention, and all activity radiates from this point. The instructor has notes or leader's guide opened before him or her and the lecture proceeds along predetermined lines. Occasionally there will be chalkboard work, but most often the teacher migrates back to the lectern as soon as the work is finished, and stays there until the next trip out. There may be some class discussion, in which case the instructor camps at the lectern for the duration of it. As the discussion progresses, the instructor remains the focal point, and generally is also in on exchanges between students. The instructor may even feel that the class is getting out of hand if the discussion is not being guided. Of course, he or she may not even allow questions or discussion because of a commitment to *cover* a certain amount of material. It may be asked that questions be held until later, although time may run out before "later" ever comes.

At the end of what has been predominantly a lecture, there may be a quiz or a test of some kind. Almost without exception the *trainees* are tested and the results show how well they have done. Indeed, the grades may be fed back to their supervisors and made a permanent part of their personnel file. Seldom, however, is the *instructor* considered in the testing. If a class does not do well, *even though the instructor is at fault,* the grades still hold and the report fails to show "Poor Teacher."

IS THE INSTRUCTOR ACCOUNTABLE FOR THE LEARNING?

Conventional teaching procedures build all the activity around the instructor, *but the students are accountable for the results.* Even if no grades go back with them, they still are shown as having attended the course, and they are expected to use the information acquired in that course on their jobs.

Many studies have been made that show how little we remember of what we hear. Yet when typical supervisors start on their teaching assignments they spend most of their preparation time on their *lecture.* Accepting even a conservative figure, we know that *after two days the student will forget at least 75 % of what he or she hears.* This fact alone should frighten a prospective instructor into looking for something besides a lecture to reinforce points. Yet we may still find the instructor reading off facts and figures,

names and descriptions, as though each trainee was going to remember every word that was said. Many a chalkboard stays un-
used while the instructor reels off innumerable statistics and
percentages. A good rule to follow is, "if it's worth remembering, it's worth presenting so it will be remembered."

Instructors should be willing to account not only for the content of everything they say and do, but for the manner in which
it is presented. It's not enough to say "the trainees don't really
have to remember this, but they ought to hear it anyway."
Statements such as this reflect a lack of understanding of the
trainees' point of view. Instructors may become so engrossed in
their subject matter and its presentation that they forget to
think in terms of the student. The preplanning, the preparation
of the leader's guides, the collection of training aids, all tend to
cause instructors to forget the reason they have a class. In fact,
the trainee becomes almost an unwanted addition, and as some
have joked, "Teaching would be all right if it weren't for the
students." But the classroom exists *because* of students; every activity should center around their need to learn. The instructor
should not decide what to do or what not to do without first
considering what problems the student may have, both in the
class and back on the job.

When an employee is taken off of his or her job and sent to
take a course, it is because the company will benefit if the employee acquires a certain body of knowledge. Supervisors who
go in as instructors must remember that their responsibility to
do a good job extends to the company, as well as to themselves
and the trainee. And in this case to do a good job means to see
that the students get what they were sent for, i.e., the information the supervisor has to impart. Some finite part of the bottom
line is at stake. *No responsible supervisor can be satisfied when a
classroomful of employees leaves his or her classroom with only a portion of
what they were supposed to learn.*

Exercises and Questions

1. Students have been heard to say, "I hope I get Mr. Jones instead of Mr. Smith because Mr. Jones is a lot easier than Mr.
   Smith." Discuss all the implications of this statement. What
   determines whether a teacher is "hard" or "easy"?

2. Teachers have been heard to say, "My job is to put it out; the student's job is to get it. I'll do my part if they'll do theirs." Discuss the implications of this statement. Have a vote to see how the group feels about who has the most responsibility—in a job situation—to see that maximum learning takes place in the classroom.

3. A supervisor called upon to teach her specialty expressed the following opinion about the responsibility for learning. "I learned mine the hard way. They didn't have any classes when I started on this job. We had to learn it or get out! I think it would be wrong for me to spoonfeed these new employees by using visual aids or anything that looks like we are begging them to learn the subject. After all, if they don't learn it, it's their tough luck. They'll be the ones to suffer when raise and promotion time comes along." Discuss the "rightness" and "wrongness" of what she is saying.

4. Try to get an idea of what it would cost to train 20 people in the organization represented in your classroom. Include salaries of the students (assume one week of training) and the instructors, as well as overhead, travel, material costs, etc. Now decide just how effective you think your training really is, that is, do the students take away 100% of what is available, 75%, 50%, or just how much? Based on the cost figures just arrived at, how much money is *lost* as a result of poor or inefficient training in your organization?

chapter 3
THE LEARNING PROCESS

People learn for many reasons, and both the amount learned and the ability to use what is learned vary with the original reason for learning. Employees fresh from a job assignment learn for reasons entirely different from those of a child in elementary school, or even those of a young adult in college. The employee tends to think in terms of the *immediate* application of new knowledge, whereas the younger student in the academic world usually thinks of the *future*. A supervisor attending a course on "how to supervise" relates what he or she learns to the job at hand, thinking of specific supervision problems, and mentally applies suggested remedies to the problems of his own back-on-the-job environment.

WHY DO PEOPLE ATTEND CLASSES?

As was pointed out earlier, we tend to teach as we have been taught. But most of our student experience was as children, not adult employees. If we go into an adult-to-adult relationship and teach as if we were in an adult-to-child situation, the trainees will quickly resist our efforts. Children may play the dependent role and accept certain things just because the teacher says them, but the adult employee is not likely to accept much on the unsupported word of the instructor.

Employees come to class with at least some experience and probably some knowledge of the subject to be taught. They expect to be treated as adults and will strongly resent it if the instructor talks down to them. They don't resent the fact that the instructor knows more about the subject than they do, but they expect to be able to grasp the information. They will become

16

extremely frustrated if the instructor wastes time talking at length in technical terms that are over the students' heads. Students are not impressed by the instructor's knowledge if that instructor fails to impart any of it. The frustrations of the trainees stem not just from being adult, but from their adult responsibilities. They may be separated from their family during the training period, they may know that no one is doing their job while they are away, and that work will be piled up, waiting for them, or they may fear that they will be held responsible for knowledge they aren't getting.

Contrary to some beliefs, the adult employee is *not* always highly motivated. The fact that trainees are adults does not mean that they will hang onto every word spoken by the instructor, nor that they will willingly endure long lectures, poor ventilation, and inept instructors. Even knowing that the subject they are studying relates to their job back home doesn't shorten a long, dull, monotonous lecture, nor does it soften a hard, uncomfortable chair.

To repeat: People learn for many and complex reasons. The supervisor may find the trainees are in his or her course because:

1. they are sent, or
2. they asked to come, or
3. "everyone is taking this course."

Those that were sent may have been sent because they:

1. can't do the work, or
2. can be spared, or
3. have the most seniority, or
4. have the least seniority, or
5. asked to come.

Those that asked to come may have done so because they:

1. want to learn, or
2. want to get away from the job, or
3. feel it is a prestige assignment, or
4. think that "everyone else is coming."

"Everyone else is coming" to the class because:

1. it is valuable learning experience, or
2. course objectives do not clearly state who should attend, or
3. top management has decreed it.

Those that want to learn may want to learn because they:

1. are curious, or
2. don't like *not knowing* something, or
3. want to do a better job, or
4. believe that doing a better job will earn them more money,

and so it goes.

Regardless of the reasons for the trainees' presence, the reason for the instructor's presence is to see that learning takes place. The learning process is complex, but it can have a simple definition for the supervisor. *Defining* it in simple forms doesn't make it a less complex procedure, however.

WHY SET OBJECTIVES?

Assuming that the course being taught was developed because there are employees who cannot properly perform their jobs, the result of learning in this case would be the ability to perform satisfactorily on the job. So learning means acquiring the ability to do something that one could not do before (including, of course, being able now to perform a given task differently or correctly). This does not necessarily refer to manual skill; it may be the ability to relate certain facts in a proper sequence to make a correct decision. It may mean being able to ferret out facts and relate them in such a way as to pass judgement on something or someone. In any event, it is the trainee's ability to do a thing that becomes important. It is this ability we should strive to develop. Our objectives (see Chapter 6) should list what we want the *learner to be able to do,* not what we want to teach.

The task becomes easier to define when we specify the degree of skill we want students to have when they leave our course.

Supervisors should never set foot in a classroom without first asking themselves, "What do I want them to be able to do when I get through with my training session?" If they can answer this realistically, then they have something by which to measure their own performance. At the end of the class period, they should ask themselves the obvious follow-up question, "Can they do what I wanted them to be able to do?"

That question is not as easy to answer correctly as it might seem. The fact that students can feed back the information presented to them by the instructor does *not* mean that they can *apply* that information. For example: The objective of a lesson is to teach the *operation* of the framus machine, for which there are ten steps. At the end of the class period every trainee can *name* the steps. Has the proper learning taken place? Not unless the trainees can *apply* these steps to the successful operation of the framus machine. Another example might be a course set up to "teach problem solving," at the end of which employees can name the steps in problem solving, i.e., define problem, get ideas, test ideas, etc. But can they then solve problems? Probably not. It may be that they have only learned to feed back the steps, not to perform the process itself. So the instructor needs to spell out in very specific and realistic terms the performance expected from the trainees, or they may end up short of the desired goal.

HOW CAN WE KNOW WHERE THE STUDENT IS NOW?

It is important for instructors to know what their trainees know and can do when they finish the course. But it is just as important for instructors to know what trainees know and can do when they first come to them. As has been pointed out, the trainees will be bored if instructors start too far below their level and frustrated if they start over their heads. It is important, then, for instructors to know when they get their trainees how well informed they are on the subject to be taught. One obvious way to find out is to test each person coming to the course. This may or may not be practicable. A better way is to give the class a test when the course begins. Unfortunately, the results may be hard to evaluate in a hurry. Also, whatever the results, the in-

structor may not be able to adjust the training program if the beginning knowledge of the class members is too uneven.

Of course, it is much better for the instructor and the trainees, and therefore for the company, if the trainees in the class all begin with the same level of information about the subject they are to study. The simplest way to ensure this is to specify in the stated objective what the trainees' achievement level should be when they *start* the course as well as what it should be when they *finish* it, and to admit to the course only those who have reached the beginning level. Trainees who are not at the proper level may prepare for the class by first taking a self-study course. A *good* programed-instruction text is ideal, because the terminal behavior will be clearly spelled out in the objective. Criterion tests will be available also, thus giving additional information to the instructor regarding each trainee's level of knowledge.

WHO IS RESPONSIBLE FOR LEARNING?

Of course, the easiest thing for the instructor to do is just to ignore the initial behavior of the trainees and start off at the level at which he or she *thinks* they should be. As bad as this sounds, it happens time and again when the instructor does not accept responsibility for what the students learn. Perhaps the least excusable attitude is that of the instructor who feels, "It's their job that's at stake, not mine, so it's their responsibility to see that they learn. I'll put it out; it's up to them to get it." Certainly no supervisor would allow an assembly line or production shop of any kind to be run with this attitude. He or she would never put out instructions at the office with such a lack of care for the results.

The point is simple: *When the supervisor becomes an instructor, the job is to teach.* He or she has the same responsibility for results in the classroom as for results back on the job.

Exercises and Questions

1. With the trainees divided into two subgroups, let one group make a list of the characteristic attitudes toward learning they think college freshmen have, and the other group make a list of the characteristics of a new employee who is a college graduate. Record these lists side by side on the board and discuss the similarities and differences. If the attitudes are different, should our approach as instructors be different? Why?

2. Now have the same two groups work on a different problem. Let one group be new first-line supervisors, promoted from within the ranks, and the other half be a group of long-service employees who are still on first-line jobs. Determine the typical attitude that would probably prevail in the classroom with these groups and report back to the whole class as in Question 1. What should our approach be in instructing each of these categories of people? Suppose they came together in the same class?

3. How important is it for the instructor to know how much the students know of the subject matter when they come to class? How can he or she *know* how much knowledge they have?

4. It is important for students to know where they are going in a course, that is, what they will be able to do when the course is over? (Answers that begin with "Well, it just depends . . . " are disqualified.)

5. On a *secret honest* ballot, determine why each student is in this particular class right now, working on this particular question. How close are these reasons to the reasons the employees would give in a typical course they would be taking?

chapter 4
LOOKING AT THE STUDENT

In Chapter 3, we made a comparison between the adult employee as a student and the growing child as a student. Now let's see how the adult employee compares with the adult academic student as a learner. The answer is significant to the supervisor as a teacher only because of the previously mentioned tendency of instructors to imitate earlier teaching examples.

IS THE INDUSTRIAL STUDENT DIFFERENT FROM THE ACADEMIC STUDENT?

The most significant difference we see is that the employee is in class for a much shorter period, usually only a matter of days. This means the subject matter cannot be as extensive as it can be in a quarter or semester of school work. The instructors, then, will have to plan their time accurately. They will have to weigh the importance of each subject carefully to determine just how much time can be allotted to it, and even eliminate it altogether if time is too short. They will have to determine whether traditional subjects justify the time customarily given them. They may discover that a certain subject is no longer needed as part of the curriculum, or they may find that what was once a minor subject is now vital to the employee's job and deserves more time. Whatever they find, one thought should prevail; *If the subject is to be taught, will there be time for the subject taught to affect the trainee's behavior?*

There is another significant time difference between the academic and industrial educational situations. The industrial class meets for *fewer days but longer days.* It is not unusual for the employee to attend an all-day session, and in many cases with the same instructor. So where the academic instructor prepares an hour's presentation, the industrial instructor usually prepares for a much longer period. This has a decided influence on both the student and the instructor.

While the longer session has the advantage of giving instructors time to properly develop their subject, it may also make them sloppy with their time. If they decide to get off the subject and "chase a few rabbits," they do so by rationalizing that there is still plenty of time. But what often happens in such cases is that the actual subject matter gets treated only in the last minutes of the class, and then very hurriedly. *The students get cheated out of time that was allotted to them to learn their job better, and the company loses x-number of man-hours of employee time.*

The longer class period works a hardship on the trainees many times because they do not get the relief of an hourly change of instructors. Of course, if the instructors are good (and they should be!) the students are satisfied not to change, but it takes alert and conscientious instructors to maintain student-involvement and their own enthusiasm for a prolonged period. It can be done, and if the students are to go away having met the prestated objectives, *it has to be done.*

WHAT DOES THE STUDENT LOOK LIKE?

Employees are geared to the present, though the future may well be in their minds. They respond best to things that relate to their jobs. Instructors who have not experienced what the employee experiences on the job, or who have been long removed from day-to-day job activities, find themselves at a disadvantage with the employee. The trainees prefer to hear references that fit their own situations, but if the training is for a future assignment, they will try to identify with that future assignment. (Academic students are in the same category, of course, except that, lacking the present experience, they may not be able to identify as well with the future assignment.)

There are times when employees will attend classes which are geared to teach theory or subjects not related to the job. How do they perform as semi-academic students? Well, they probably have several things going against them, especially if the course is a rigorous one. They will most likely be out of the habit of regular, sustained study assignments. They will not be accustomed to reading and reciting, that is, giving an account of their previous night's study. They will not be in the habit of competing with others in a classroom situation. Add to this their concern for their families and the personal problems that are a part of the daily routine, and it sounds pretty bad for them as students. But they have some things going for them which may more than offset these handicaps.

They are mature adults and are able to accept the fact that they are expected to learn the material. While they haven't been in the habit of studying, they are used to reading mail, company reports, specification sheets, and/or other things that require meticulous study and understanding. Even though it has been some time since they have had to give an account of their studying, there has rarely been a day that they haven't had to stand behind a decision they made as a result of reading such material. The same is true regarding competition with others. In meetings, conferences, reporting sessions, and on the job with employees, they compete by defending their position before other departments, the boss, or their peers. So you see, they are not total strangers to the rigors of classwork. We do them an injustice when we say they've been out of school so long they can't take it. College professors who have had much experience with industrial students prefer them to the regular college student for the reasons listed above.

IS THERE A STUDENT STEREOTYPE?

While we are describing the characteristics of employees as students, we should ask if they have a stereotype. The things listed as *typical* of the employee are just that, *typical.* They do not describe every trainee, nor do all trainees have even some of the characteristics. We can only describe *in general* what the trainee will be like, but *this is important* to the *instructor.* There are those who would put all employee-students into one category. (And the category differs, of course, depending on who's doing the categorizing.) Just as instructors differ, so do students. By the time a class is assembled, it will be made up of several different kinds of employees. They will differ greatly in experience with the company, educational background (both in attainment and quality), social background, and motivation. These things may not work against the instructor, but he or she should be aware that they exist.

It is not enough to select only employees with some quality common to all of them, i.e., age, present job, length of service, etc. Even then they will not be alike as students. One has only to look at a class of graduating college seniors or a group of newly hired personnel to realize that even under close environmental similarity the individuals are quite different. But these differences needn't frighten supervisors as instructors. They are used to seeing people with different backgrounds and personalities adjust to similar tasks without causing unnecessary problems. And so it is with a classroom situation; as long as they fit the description in the objectives (stating what they should know by now) instructors can expect little or no trouble from these differences. In fact, variety of backgrounds *will probably add to the value of the course if the instructors are wise enough to use it.*

One difference with which instructors should concern themselves is the matter of *why* the employees are taking the course. As mentioned in Chapter 3, they will learn for different reasons. Those who are naturally curious will be more highly motivated than those who feel they are being forced to learn. Those who are taking the course as a means of getting ahead may try to dominate the discussion for their own benefit, while those who are willing to learn as a part of their employee obligation may not attempt to get into the discussion at all. Instructors cannot set themselves up as judges of motives, but experience will tell them when they have a problem. One sure warning sign is when one person does all the talking (including the instructor!), or when one or two never participate at all. It may be all right for the one class. Some people naturally talk out more than others, and some are naturally quiet. There are ways of regulating both situations, as we will see in Chapter 9, but we are talking here about the "dominator" and the "withdrawer."

TYPES OF STUDENTS

We have just pointed out that there are no stereotypes for students, but there are some *types* of students. Fortunately, we can find certain categories of students so we can figure out how to deal with each type. Generally, students fall into one of three categories, as far as their approach to learning is concerned. Any one student may change categories, depending upon the course, the circumstances, the reports from students who have previously attended the same course, the attitude of the supervisor toward training, and so on. Let's look at the three general categories, though, and see how we deal with each.

First, there is the student—the employee—who sees learning as an opportunity to advance in the organization. There is a chance of getting ahead with certain knowledge, so the employee feels it's important to learn whatever is put out. The goal is not the learning, but what the learning can bring about for the student. But since learning has to come first, the student is willing to buckle down and learn. How do we deal with students like this? We make plenty of reference to the application of the material being learned to the jobs back home. Since these learners aren't going to get too excited about just getting quantities of information, they'll be more interested in their success as it relates to being able to get or do the job they're looking at. For these learners, learning is a means of getting to a goal, not a goal in itself.

Next, there is the employee who is turned on by learning *just for the sake of learning.* This is the student who likes to attend any course that's offered, brags about how many have been attended, and enjoys learning. This, too, will be a good student, but the motivation here has got to be an opportunity to learn. *These students must know they're learning.* Feedback on learning is the key to success for the instructors and the students when we have these learners in class. We may find that they aren't too motivated when we talk about application on the job. We find them sitting on the edges of their seats when we get into the technical aspects of the subject—even if it's abstract and seemingly unrelated to the job back home. If the course turns out to be too basic, or a review of previously learned information, we may find them becoming uninterested, withdrawing, or even disrupting with more technical questions than we plan on. The best hope for us in situations like this is to use these people's knowledge to teach others. These students have fairly high retention of the subject matter they've studied, and we meet their ego needs by calling on them to share this knowledge. This keeps them interested, gives us a chance to get a little more involvement from the students, and builds credibility into the material being taught.

Finally, there is the student who just likes to be around people who are learning. The "academic" background is pleasing for this student, and it is more of a social thing than a need to learn, or meet a goal. Like the learners who liked learning for learning's sake, these people also like to go to courses, but more for the social benefits than the learning. Obviously this student has had some success at learning or the environment wouldn't be so appealing, so *capability* does exist. There is probably some motivation, too, so we won't have to work too hard getting this person to learn. Note, though, that while this person is interested in the social relationships that take place in a learning situation, the first type we mentioned is not at all interested in this aspect. The learner who is looking for something beyond the learning usually wants the teacher to "get on with it," and may listen closely to a lecture, watch a film intently, or work independently for as long as it takes to get the job done. This "social" learner, on the other hand, would much prefer to be in small subgroups, talking, exchanging ideas, solving problems in a *group mode,* rather than in a self-study activity.

We wouldn't want to suggest that all students are easily identifiable and recognizable as to type the moment we see them. Perhaps we'll never be able to recognize and categorize some of them. But that's all right. Knowing that these types exist in almost every class, we do our teaching to appeal to *all three types.* We have some challenge for the person who wants to learn, enjoys learning, and is very motivated just by learning. We have ample application sessions for those who are concerned about the job back home and about future jobs that this learning experience can lead to. We don't make promises; we just talk about how this can be used in different ways. For the learner who enjoys the learning environment from a social standpoint, there is the frequent accumulation of people into work groups, *with meaningful activities,* for interaction in a social/learning situation.

HOW DO WE DEAL WITH THE "DOMINATOR"?

In his anxiety to get class participation, the instructor will welcome discussion. Unfortunately, though, this encourages the "dominator" to take over, and sooner or later the instructor will have to deal with him or her. The group may begin to "punish" the dominator after a while, but not before valuable time has been wasted. The dominator places the instructor in a delicate position. The instructor must not stifle discussion, nor create a "threat level" that will discourage future participation. Also, the instructor must make sure that this particular student is trying to press for personal gain. It would be a serious mistake to squelch the dominator if he or she is really a serious student trying to learn. *Remember, until proven otherwise, every trainee must be treated as though wanting to learn.*

If indeed, however, the trainee is only interested in being heard or in impressing the instructor, action must be taken. But what action? If the instructor cuts off all discussion, the serious students are silenced along with the dominator. If the instructor indicates to the problem student displeasure with that student's behavior the threat level rises sharply, and the group may even feel an urge to protect one of its own members. One subtle approach is for the instructor to call on specific people by name. This will give others a chance to participate and will discourage the dominator. A subtler method is for the instructor to have each person *write* the answers to a question asked, then ask the students to check with their neighbors. After a minute or two, the instructor may ask the *neighbors* of the problem student what they came up with. If the dominator cuts in, the instructor may calmly wait for an opening, then ask the *neighbor*, "Is that what you had?" If the dominator continues to be a problem, a word in private will generally be sufficient.

The question always arises, "Why not deal outright with this troublemaker?" The answer is simply that the class is made up of adults, not children. They will not accept a strong, forceful treatment because they feel that they are pretty much on the same level as the instructor. They expect a supportive, even informal, climate, and a feeling of mutual respect between themselves and the instructor. The instructor must be extremely careful not to develop a competitive spirit between himself or herself and the class. *The students must always feel that the instructor is there to help them learn, not to joust with them.*

THE WITHDRAWER

The problem of the "withdrawer" differs from that of the dominator, but it is equally challenging. The student who remains a nonparticipant is often overlooked because of not interfering in any way. To the conscientious instructor, however, this student stands out as much as or more than the dominator. The withdrawer is giving no feedback, no evidence of either interest or learning. We're not referring to the shy trainee, but to the one who neither talks nor appears to listen, who may even show signs of disinterest or rebellion. What should the instructor do about this student?

The first impulse of the instructor, especially if he or she is delivering long lectures, may be to ignore such a student. The second impulse may be to embarrass the student into participation. Of course, this may cause more withdrawal, and it may cause the rest of the class to resent the instructor. Now, the instructor does not have time to solve whatever problems may be bothering the withdrawer, yet there is the responsibility to see that each student learns. Therefore the withdrawer must be urged to participate in *spite* of personal problems.

The best approach is to force the withdrawer to participate in a nonthreatening situation. A good way to do this is to have the group work on some simple task by tables or in groups of two. The exercise need only last two or three minutes—just long enough to force the withdrawer to participate. Then the instructor goes round the room and, at each table, requests one person—by *name*—to tell the answers. At the withdrawer's table, the withdrawer is called on by name, to make comment. The instructor may say, for example, "What would happen if we failed to do this step first?" By answering, the withdrawer becomes a participating member of the discussion, but not in an obviously embarrassing way. The instructor should keep the withdrawer's comments in mind, however, for future use in pulling him or her back into the group.

Of course, a casual discussion with the withdrawer at lunch or during a break may reveal some of the things causing trouble. If so, then so much the better. Don't be afraid of such questions as, "Well, what do you think of the course so far?" or, "Do you think there's anything here that you can use back on the job?" The answers may not please you, but they may help in dealing with the problem. We don't want to pit ourselves against one or more trainees. *We are not in the classroom to compete with the students.*

This pitting of the student against the instructor is a serious matter, and it often happens before the instructor is aware of it. Teachers have long known that classes have personalities just as do individuals. One group will be outspoken, noisy, perhaps full of humor and pranks. The next may be quiet, studious, even sullen. There isn't much the instructor can do to change this, but he or she should be wise enough to spot it, for it will definitely affect the learning habits of the group. The instructor will have to adjust to the class personality if possible, because what works with one group may not work with another. Since one group may laugh at anything and the next group may not laugh at all, even the use of humor will have to vary. A group that is boisterous may have to be brought back under control frequently, while the more sedate groups may need some livening up.

Sometimes the personality of a group can be traced to one or two "ringleaders." If it is a serious problem, a private talk with the individuals involved will help solve it. If there are only one or two who are upsetting the group, the members of the group may themselves take steps to "tone down" the troublemakers. This is fine, unless their action is too severe, in which case there may be serious arguments.

The instructor is concerned with such things because they affect the object of the course—to teach. The purpose of the course is to change the behavior of the trainee in certain ways. Anything, everything, that will hinder the reaching of this goal is the business of the instructor.

THE "I'D RATHER BE HOME" STUDENT

In almost every session we conduct we find at least one student who gives us the impression, "I'd rather be at home than here in this class." We are fortunate if we do not have such a student, but also fortunate if we have one and know *for sure* that is the attitude. Many students give that appearance, but we read them incorrectly, for they may have some other problem too. This is likely to cause some mistakes if we act too hastily. Sometimes students are frightened at being away from home in a strange environment with people they don't know, studying material they don't feel comfortable with. As a protection for themselves, they give an "I don't care" appearance. They really do care. They really do want to learn. They really hope they do well and get a good report when they go home. But we can't always read between the lines, and sometimes we make a poor judgment as to the reason for the actions of the student.

If, however, we do have a student who is obviously not interested in being in the course, but would, in fact, rather be at home, what do we do? Let's assume that sending the student home is not a very good solution. We'll assume that there are reasons why the student needs to be there. There is a deficiency in his or her performance, and the decision to send this person was a good one. There are several approaches we can take. We can try to find out why the person doesn't want to be there. There's a good chance that there was a poor selling job back home by the supervisor. Perhaps the supervisor failed to point out the deficiency properly, so that the student is not aware of anything being wrong. Or, at the other extreme, maybe the boss laid it on the line, "Learn this or you've had it!" The student is faced with the dilemma of taking the course, failing and taking the consequences, or not taking the course, and postponing the consequences. It may be that the student is losing money by being here, because of some quota system or commission arrangement whereby money is being lost during the training. (Note that we can't correct these inequities right now in this class, though we might be able to make some recommendations for future sessions.) Another reason may be that the student feels that being sent to this course is degrading in some way. He or she may feel that this is going to be a waste of time, with all this information already being committed to use back on the job. There may be other reasons, and we may not be able to find out what they are. But if we do, we can make some adjustments and bring out some points that will help this student overcome the undesirable feelings.

What can we do? First, we use the basic motivating tool we should use with all our students to get and keep them interested: we try to show them *what's in it for them.* Another way to get them with us with more concern is to appeal to the recognition, or status, principle of motivation. If the employee brings certain skills or some stored up knowledge, rather than seeing it as a threat to us, we should use it to give recognition and status to the student. "Fran, you've had some good experience in this field . . . would you share it with us as it pertains to this particular problem?" This way we not only get the student recognition, but get some feedback on just where the student really is at this time.

Closely related to what we've just said is another method of encouraging trainees who don't want to be there to become more of a part of the training program. This is to ask these people to find relevancy in what we're saying. It asks them to give inputs on just what this course can provide the learner back on the job. This tends to make the students researchers for us, but it doesn't require an expert to find the answer. Even if the employee is one of those who feels inadequate or behind the rest of the group, looking for relevancy will be a good source of encouragement. It's a subtle way of having employees find the reasons for the course being run in the first place, and finding their own weaknesses may explain why their bosses sent them to the course at this particular time.

If there seems to be a number of students who fall in this "don't want to be there" category, it may be best to call a halt to planned activity and let the class as a whole consider the advantages and timeliness of the course being run at this time. This will get some of the "I'm glad I'm here" students working for us and doing a little persuasion for us. It could be that these students can do more to bring reality and need to the course than we can.

Finally, we haven't mentioned the obvious thing that can be done, and that's to have a private talk with the trainee and see if there's anything we need to know that would make the course more valuable to this person, and maybe to the class as a whole. This shouldn't be a "jump all over the trainee" session. All we need to do is to start a conversation with "How's it going?" and follow good interviewing techniques from there on. If we don't succeed this way, we may be more pointed and say, "I get the feeling that I'm not making this course as valuable to you as I'd like to. Is there something else I need to be doing?" We aren't trying to put the trainees on the spot, nor start a war with them. What we really want to do is find out how we can help the employee be a more valuable one. Since we believe there is a need for this information and skill being learned by the employee, we want to help both the organization and the employee by making this happen.

Exercises and Questions

1. With the class divided in two groups, have one group be students in a typical classroom in your organization. This group should make a list of all the problems they have with instructors. The other half are instructors in a typical classroom. They should make a list of all the problems they have with students in their classes. When this information is put on the board, discuss the reasons for the difference in attitudes that exist between the students and teachers. Should the teacher take this difference into consideration when teaching?

2. Still looking at the lists from Question 1, see how many of the problems are "self-oriented," that is, are problems that come about as a result of trying to make the situation fit "my own convenience." Discuss ways of turning the problems into advantages from a learning standpoint.

3. Make a list of all the possible reasons why an employee-student would try to do all the talking in a classroom. Now make a similar list of all the reasons why an employee-student would not talk at all in class. Does it really matter to the teacher why the person does or does not talk in class? What can be done to overcome each of these two situations?

4. Discuss the idea that classes have personalities. How can this personality affect the learning process?

5. Are some of the people in *this* class talking more than others? Why? Is it harmful to the learning of the total group? Has the instructor tried to do anything about getting the quieter ones to speak up?

chapter 5
COMMUNICATION: TOOL OF THE TRADE

The teaching-learning process is more than just the transmission of words from the instructor to the student. Good teaching requires that the *proper* words be transmitted, and that these words convey useful information, i.e., concepts, direction, etc. In turn, the student must do more than just passively receive words; he or she must interpret them and relate them to job requirements.

WHY DO WE USE WORDS?

We do most of our communicating by arranging words into sequences which convey meaning. The instructor's mind contains information which is encoded into words. These words are

transmitted by the voice mechanism through the air to the ear of the student, and thence to the brain. The student's brain, acting as a computer, *decodes* the words in terms of previously known information. If the message said "black box," the student's brain reacts to the color "black," and a configuration of a "box." Since there are *little* black boxes, and *big* black boxes, the student still does not have the total picture, but has registered a general concept.

If the instructor's message said "burple widgit," the student's brain would not register a decoded concept. Nothing in the students "computer store" reacts with the words "burple" or "widget." On the other hand, if the instructor had shown a picture *labeled* "burple widgit," the student could have received the information. Pictures usually bypass a good portion of the encoding and decoding process, hence lead to better understanding. (Of course it could be argued that even a picture is a code, since only a *real* horse is a horse, but for our purpose this is beside the point.)

What has all of this got to do with teaching? Very much, because while instructors use words to convey their thoughts, they may not realize the importance of choosing their words carefully. Instructors should ask themselves frequently if their words are properly chosen with regard to the *learner's* vocabulary. Instructors who blandly throw out unfamiliar words or expressions are a disgrace to their calling. Sometimes supervisors try to shore up their confidence as instructors by demonstrating their command of the subject being taught. They will try to demonstrate their right to be teachers by purposely omitting explanations or using words foreign to the student's vocabulary. They may convince the class that they know a lot, but they will not build up its confidence in them, nor will the class respect them as instructors.

When two different words or expressions mean the same thing, the instructor should *use the simpler one.* This is a very sound rule which will gain the instructor the respect of the students and make the subject easier to learn. Time and again instructors fall into the trap of using complex terms to express an idea. Often they don't realize that they're doing it; the language is familiar to them so they assume that it is familiar to the student. Sometimes instructors will rationalize by saying that they

don't want to talk down to the student. They forget that if the trainees were familiar with the subject, they wouldn't need an instructor.

The teaching-learning process has been described as a process by which the transmitter (the teacher) passes information to a receiver (the student). The transmitter determines how much information should be sent and received in a given length of time, what may be considered satisfactory results, and when they have been achieved. The receiver, on the other hand, is trying to determine how much work should be put in to receive all that is sent, what should be learned, and how to know when it has been learned.

Now we have an interesting phenomenon: the instructor is trying to tune in on the *learner's input,* and the learner is trying to tune in on the *instructor's output.* The degree to which *each* of them successfully tunes in the other determines the success of the teaching-learning effort!

CAN THE INSTRUCTOR PREVENT LEARNING?

In this transmitting-receiving process the instructor still carries the prime responsibility. If the instructor operates on too high a frequency the student may find it impossible to stay tuned in without having more background knowledge or greater learning

ability. If the instructor operates on too low a frequency, the student may find it impossible to stay tuned in without being bored to death. Visual aids will be discussed later at greater length; for now, it's worth mentioning that while a *good* picture beats a lot of words, a *bad* picture may actually reduce learning and is rarely a substitute for any kind of words. New instructors are sometimes convinced that visuals are necessary, and feel that they should never speak without having some visual aid in front of the students at all times. It often happens, though, that the pictures or other visual aids don't really relate to the subject at hand, and the students still get the same dull lecture. The instructor may think he or she is doing fine, and get quite a shock when turning on the lights to find the group asleep. One picture on a screen should never be taken as a license for a half-hour lecture. If the picture has enough information on it to allow the instructor to talk for more than just a few minutes, it must be too cluttered for the student to see clearly or understand!

HOW CAN THE INSTRUCTOR BEST COMMUNICATE?

When the student and his or her problems become the foremost consideration of the instructor, much of the battle is won. The instructor, in trying to tune in the student, must ask himself or herself many questions:

1. Where is the student now?

What does he or she know, what skills does he or she have or lack? What information and misinformation has the student brought to class? How does the student compare with each of the other learners?

2. How can *this* student and *this* group best learn?

What factors will determine their progress? How long has it been since they have attended a class and/or studied extensively? Can they concentrate for long periods or do they need frequent breaks?

3. What is my role as instructor of *this* class?

Am I a helper or a leader? Is the group looking for guidance to improve a skill, or are they learning something for the first time? Are they young and willing to accept me as instructor, or are they experienced and willing to question my position?

These questions must be faced before the instructor can correctly teach the student. Time and again instructors should ask themselves, "Am I directing my efforts to produce learning or am I just using up time? Do I know all I should know about these students in order to cause the necessary learning?" If they face these questions squarely, communications barriers will start to vanish.

PROVIDING A HANDLE

If instructors want to communicate properly, they will organize materials and presentations in a realistic manner. They must give the students a "handle" by which to locate themselves. By this we mean simply that students need something to which they can tie their new information, namely some information they already have, or a concept they already understand, or a skill they have seen performed before. In other words, the presentation that means the most to the student is the one that starts with "This is similar to . . . " or "Picture in your mind a . . . " or "The same parts are used . . . " From that point the instructor presents new information, always associating it with something the student already knows. *The student gets from the known to the unknown by a bridge of related facts.* The instructor who expects the student to correctly unite a series of seemingly unrelated facts does that student no favor.

THE STUDENT NEEDS THE BIG PICTURE

One obstacle to effective communication by instructors is the fact that *they know too much.* They see the "big picture," the overall scope of things, and yet must communicate with someone who lacks this advantage. To illustrate this, draw a simple configuration of squares and rectangles or triangles, then try to describe it to someone who cannot see it. This is a difficult task, because while you, the viewer, see the whole configuration, you must describe it to someone who does not know where even one line is. Similarly, the instructors (the viewer) will omit some information because it is difficult for them to know how little the student understands of the overall goal.

Here again it is necessary for instructors to put themselves in the student's place. The student must know how the information given in class fits the total objective of the course, otherwise he or she is like someone who has a few random pieces of a jigsaw puzzle but no idea of what the total puzzle looks like. Yet instructors may repeat this mistake again and again by *assuming* that the students know where they are going.

One of the most dangerous pitfalls in the teaching process is to *assume that the student knows or can do a specific thing.* Instructors should build a body of knowledge step by step in logical order. In such a process, each step is dependent on the preceding one. But occasionally instructors may think, "surely the students know this," so they skip that step and go to the next one. By assuming that the students know one of the steps, instructors have jeopardized their understanding of all the following steps. The time it would have taken instructors to check their assumption would have been time well spent. Again it would have helped to have placed themselves in the learner's chair.

It is not enough, either, to assume that because one person knows a certain fact, everyone does. Even experienced instructors can be trapped by the student who appears to answer for the whole class, saying, "Oh, we've had that before." This causes the instructor to think that everyone understands the point, and the rest of the group may not be willing to admit their ignorance. But the rule is simple: when raising a point on which succeeding facts or points depend, *check it out before going on!*

Exercises and Questions

1. With the group divided into two subgroups, see which can come up with the longest list of "Barriers to Communication," whether in a classroom or in a conversation between two people. Record the various barriers on the board. Have

the group vote on the three most often raised by a *new* instructor. Would an instructor with more experience raise different barriers?

2. Using the list from Question 1, have the group decide which barriers can occur in the classroom. Now check which ones can be raised *without* the instructor's knowing it. What can be done to avoid these "unconscious" barriers from interfering with learning?

3. "Meaningful learning cannot take place unless the learner can associate or relate the new information to something already known." Basing the answers on this statement, why are some subjects "hard" and some subjects "easy" and how much of the difference between the two has to do with communications?

4. Discuss the statement: "One obstacle to effective communications by instructors is the fact they *they know too much.*" Give examples from the experiences of the class.

chapter 6
TASK ANALYSIS

It is perhaps unfortunate that something as important and as simple to describe (although not simple to do) should be saddled with a name as unfamiliar to the everyday supervisor as "Task Analysis." If the idea is unacceptable to some people, it must be because of the choice of words to describe the function.

But Task Analysis is just that: an analysis of the work (task) to be done. It is a vital part of the training assignment. In fact, unless it is performed with some expertise, the training job is headed for trouble. In this chapter we will look at task analysis from the standpoint of what it is, how it is done, what its significance is to the training program and to the trainer, how it can best be used and who should do it.

There are three things we need to deal with in order to understand a task analysis properly. As we'll see, task analysis is a step-by-step breakdown of the job, and a necessary thing in order for the training to be logical and systematic. There is also what we call a job description. This varies from organization to organization, but in most places it sets the *area of responsibility* for the employees. It is a statement of what decisions and work functions the employee has, and where the line is drawn between employees. Finally, there are job standards which really combine both the task analysis and the job description. The job description tells what the responsibility is, the task analysis tells what steps are to be taken to get the job done, and the job standards tell *how well* the job is to be done. As we'll see in the next chapter, the trainer must know all three of these things in order to develop a realistic set of objectives for the training program.

WHAT IS TASK ANALYSIS?

Everyone who works for an organization—any organization at all—should have a reasonably well-defined job. This is true for the president, the managers, the foremen, the production workers, and the house-service workers. We will call the operation that they do the "task," so that when we take a very close look at their job—to the point of specifying exactly, step by step, each small operation—we will be doing a *task analysis*.

A task analysis is that function that describes the work in *performance* terms rather than "end product" terms. It differs from a job description, for instance. A job description simply tells us what the end result of the performance is supposed to be. (This isn't an "always-true" statement, because there is no complete agreement on what a job description is.) For example, if we say that a production assistant in a TV studio operates a camera 60% of his or her time, we have *described* the job, but we have not *analyzed* it. With the job description alone we are unable to proceed with the training. We need to know in greater detail the actual duties that will be performed on the job before adequate training can be devised.

Let's look at some examples to get a better idea of what we are talking about when we say performance rather than end product. How would we write a job description of a waiter's or waitress's job? Reduced to the essentials, it would perhaps look like this:

1. Get the customer seated.
2. Get the customer's order.
3. Transmit the order to the kitchen.
4. Get the food to the customer.
5. Collect the money for the food.
6. Get the customer out of the restaurant.

Note that this could be the description of the waiter's or waitress's job in almost any restaurant, large or small. It is a good description of the job duties of the person handling the customer's order and getting the food to her. It would eliminate any question of "who does what around here?" But let's see how good this description is as a guide to the person doing the training.

	TASK ANALYSIS	
STEP:	**OPERATION**	
1	Go to cabinet and count out 20 copies of forms 101, 103 and 201 B.	
2	Go back to work table	
3	Open envelope	
4	Insert forms	
5	Seal envelope	
6	Place envelope in out-mail basket	

Take the first item, for instance: "Get the customer seated." What is the procedure? Do I stand at the table and motion for the customer, or do I go and meet her, then lead her through the maze of tables to the vacant one? Do I allow her to find her own table, then serve her? Do I ask her whether she has a preference or choose a table for her? Do I pick out a seat for her at the table or do I let her sit on any side she likes? Note that any one of these choices will fit the job description, but each is quite different from the other. If I'm only supervising and am concerned with job assignments, I really don't care, just so long as the job gets done according to the standard set forth by the organization. But if I'm concerned with the training—and the supervisor certainly should be—then it's imperative that I know which method is to be employed to get the customer seated. A good task analysis gives the answers to the questions asked above. It tells us the little details of the job that are vital to the training person. It gives us the information that we need to write the objectives in behavioral (or performance) terms. It provides us with the information we must have to decide what kind of training is needed, how much training we should do, and how big the training steps should be. It also gives us something to measure the *results* of our training by. With the job spelled out in the proper detail, and a good set of objectives, it is simple enough to decide whether or not the employee is doing the job as we had hoped to train him or her to do it.

We could take the rest of the job description for the waiter or waitress and ask the same questions, but let's look at some other examples. Let's take the case of a secretary. Most people seem to know what a secretary does, but in fact secretarial assignments differ in many cases. What would a partial job description look like?

1. Answer the telephones.
2. Receive or transmit information to the caller.
3. Serve as receptionist.
4. Handle the mail, both incoming and outgoing.
5. Other duties.

The job is more extensive than this, of course, but these items will give us a start. Take the first item, "Answer the phones." If that were the entire task analysis, it would be a simple matter to teach the person to do this job. If the person can tell which end of the phone to talk into and which end to listen to and knows how to say, "Hello," the training program is over already!

But that's not all there is to answering the telephone. A task analysis would go into detail, even to the extent of specifying how often the phone may ring before it must be answered. ("Answer before the third ring.") How about pleasantness? Is it important that the secretary speak distinctly? Is it necessary to identify herself to the caller? Should he give the extension number or the name of the department? Should she open with a "Good Morning!" or "Good Afternoon!" or are there other phrases she should use? Should he close the conversation with a "Thank you for calling us"? What are the rules for passing the call on to someone else in the office? Suppose the boss is busy, or has a visitor in the office? Does he attempt to help the caller or does he try to find out if the boss is willing to talk anyway? Obviously there are more questions, but these will give an idea of the depth to which the task analysis should go. And this is only one of the items in the description of the secretary's job. Some of the others are even more extensive. The matter of handling the mail, for instance, is an elaborate one, because it includes the factor of decision making. (Other items do, too, but this one especially.) Will she recognize "hot" items? Is she expected to assign work when the boss is away?

Now let's look at another example. What is the job description of a manager of a branch office? A partial list would look like this:

1. Be responsible for the hiring of personnel.
2. Handle the personnel records of all employees.
3. Handle all disciplinary problems that arise.
4. Provide a yearly evaluation of each employee.
5. Recommend salary increases of the employees.
6. Other duties.

Obviously this is only a very partial list of all the duties the manager is to perform—it does not include even the organization's relations with the customers. But it gives us a starting point for a discussion of the difference between the outline above and a task analysis of the same assignment. Any one of the items above shows the need for analyzing the job in greater detail before training is done.

For the first duty, the hiring of personnel, what would a task analysis include? It would include the techniques for recruiting people. Would a sign be placed in the window or an ad in the paper? Would there be an effort to hire people recommended by present employees, thereby requiring a special campaign? Would the manager conduct a hiring interview? Would the manager handle the completion of the necessary forms or will they be

mailed to the main office? These are small details, but if you were going to train a person to be a branch manager, it would be absolutely necessary that the person know these and other things about the hiring aspect of the job. Maybe all of these things need not be learned in a classroom, but *they will have to be learned somewhere.* Whoever is responsible for the supervision and training of these managers had better make sure that the managers have had a chance to learn the details before the job is turned over to them. By the same token, it isn't fair to evaluate the manager's performance later on if nobody recognized the need for some training in the matter of hiring people, keeping records, disciplining employees, and so on.

WHY DO A TASK ANALYSIS?

Now that we have found out *what* a task analysis is, let's see just why we need one to carry on the training job. First of all, it is essential that instructors have access to this kind of information. If they don't, they will find themselves guessing and assuming much more than they should. They may be spending valuable time on things that aren't really that important, and omitting items in the training that are essential. During the training, the instructors can see that what they are doing in their classes is parallel to what the trainee will have to do at the work location. They are able to get and hold the trainees' interest because what they are saying is directly related to and immediately usable on the job. They no longer need to guess why a certain job aspect is covered in great detail. They no longer have to *hope* that what they are doing in class is based on safe assumptions; they *know* what they are doing and why they are doing it. This offers a tremendous advantage to the student, also, for many obvious reasons.

There is another reason for doing the task analysis. *There is always a chance that the job is being done wrong now.* Many jobs don't get planned—they just evolve with the organization or with the person who is doing the work. It isn't unusual for a job to grow up around a certain man, for example, because of his abilities, and when he leaves, the next person—though not necessarily possessing the same qualities—will be expected to do the same job in the same manner. Not only does this cause difficulties in filling the job when it becomes vacant, but it gives rise to even greater difficulties in training someone who is expected to fill the vacancy. There may be no logic to the way the job is organized; there may still be a "flavor" of the first person who had the job and developed it to the point where it is today. It may be that there are other ways of doing the job that would be quicker and more profitable. It may be that we will have to take the *personality* aspect out of the job and look at it from the standpoint of the organization's needs.

Some could argue at this point that we will never be able to take all of the personality out of a job because any job is going to reflect the nature of the person doing it. This isn't bad and it isn't exactly what the problem is. The problem arises when individuals insert their personality into the steps and procedures which have been proven to get the best results. This kind of change isn't good for the organization and shouldn't be allowed to creep in. An example of this can be found in the case of the waiter or waitress mentioned earlier. If the best procedure for ensuring the restaurant's good "public image" is to approach the customer and lead her to the table, it isn't acceptable for the waiter or waitress to decide that this is too much trouble and just stand at the table until getting the attention of the customer and then waving for her to be seated. This is inserting "personality" too far. On the other hand, if he or she decides to make idle conversation about the weather while walking to the table, then that's fine. This conversational gambit is probably something that would be hard to train for and maybe we'd rather not even try to develop this technique in all our people. The task analysis would not include this bit of the job, nor would the training program.

What we are interested in finding out is whether or not the actual job—as it's laid out—is really the best way to accomplish the desired end result. This means finding out what is being done and looking at it carefully to see whether there is any way of making an improvement. If the clerk has to hit 19 keys on the cash register to ring up one charge sale, is there a way of accomplishing the same thing with fewer punches? If the office supervisor has to fill out forms in triplicate once a week to report expenditures or cash receipts, is it possible that some of this work is unnecessary? If the clerk has to make three trips to the

mail room a week to get postage, can something be done to reduce the number of trips? If all employee appraisals have to be
done by November 1, is there some way of changing the system
so that appraisals will fall on each employee's service anniversa-
ry? A good, careful task analysis may reveal a number of instances on which improvements can be made, even before the
training is done. It may even be possible that when the job is
simplified, there will be less need for training. (If the clerk is
making too many mistakes because the sales slips are a complex
Chinese Puzzle of carbons and foldovers, coming up with a simpler process may reduce the errors to the point where there is no
longer any real need for training.)

THE JOB CHANGES

One reason a job needs to be analyzed is that over the years it
changes. Not only do different people tend to introduce different ways of doing the job, but there are changes because of
technological advances. There is almost always an evolution in
the methods of doing any job, and even the desired end product
may be different from what it was a few years ago. Many training programs have been found to be obsolete because of such
changes. If a careful task analysis isn't done periodically, we
may end up training the people in a way that is completely
wrong. This is not only frustrating to the employees who go
back and find they can't use the training they have had, but it
wastes time and money for the organization. (Not to mention
the poor reputation that the employees develop for those doing
the training!)

HOW DO YOU DO A TASK ANALYSIS?

All of this brings us to an obvious point: how do you go about a
task analysis? First, it should be pointed out emphatically that
one should learn to *think small* when starting to think about a
task analysis. There is no way of performing a careful analysis
of any work operation without breaking it down into very small
bits and stages. This should be obvious from the examples given
earlier in this chapter, showing the difference between job de-

scription and task analysis. One would have a difficult time in analyzing the branch manager's job if one merely said that "the manager was responsible for the operation of the office." We've already seen that it would be impossible to put together a realistic training program with no more information than this. So a prime rule is that the person doing the task analysis must be able to break the job down into small enough segments that the actual performance can be described in detail.

Another important decision that must be made before one can prepare a satisfactory task analysis is whether or not it is to be done very formally or informally. About the only difference in the end result is the *appearance*: a task analysis done formally uses forms with rows and columns and words that are more scholarly; in an informal one, the job is described step by step in the same way, except that there is no prescribed method that must be followed by everyone doing an analysis. In either case, the important thing is the *care* with which the analysis is done. The absence of elaborate forms and instructions does not mean that the job can be done haphazardly or without much attention to detail. If there was ever a time when accuracy counted, this is it.

So the basis for doing a task analysis is to think small and decide what form the results will take. There are other ingredients, of course, but they are obvious, such as knowledge of the subject, thoroughness, use of understandable and everyday language, etc. With these in mind, the task analysis can begin. There are two processes, each with advantages and disadvantages. First, there is the procedure of "watching" someone who is now doing the job, listing the actions one by one, then letting this list be the task analysis. The advantages are obvious. The best *content specialist* should be the person who is actually doing the job. This approach saves time and energy which would have to be spent if one tried to dig into the work operation and find out how it is to be done without the aid of someone who knows just what is to be done.

The disadvantages of this procedure are just as obvious: how do we keep from building in mistakes and wrong techniques if we simply watch someone who is now doing the job? Do we know that they are doing it in the best and most up-to-date manner? Are we sure that they haven't developed some sloppy habits? These are important questions and the training shouldn't begin until they are answered. This disadvantage can be over-come by taking the observed steps as a *place to begin,* then going on from there. Looking at the work as it is now being performed tells us at least one way of accomplishing the end result, but we review our findings critically with an eye toward making im-provements. Why is the job being done this way? Why can't we accomplish the same thing some other way? Is there some inef-ficiency built into the present way of doing things? Are there duplications or omissions? Taking this approach will get much of the built-in error out of the task analysis and protect the training program.

Another approach is to start with the end product or desired end result and figure out the best way to get to that point. This is done initially without watching someone perform the task. There should be a person present who knows something about the job but this person shouldn't be allowed to say "This is the way it is being done now." After the job has been defined in terms of end results, then it is time to go and look at someone performing the task. When there are differences between the way it seems the job should be done if one looks at the end re-sult and the way it is now being done, judgment is used to de-cide which is, in fact, the best way of reaching the goal. Here, again, the advantages are obvious. We have a plan of work that removes some of the prejudices of "That's the way we've always done it." We have allowed imagination to suggest ways of ac-complishing something that may have been going on for many years in a rather unimaginative manner. The critical part of this method is to make sure that the judgment used in making the decisions on the best way of performing the task are sound judgments, unprejudiced if at all possible

The disadvantage to this method is that it takes more time and that imagination may not be available. Also, the people working on the project may be so familiar with the job that they cannot look at the operation without seeing how the existing workers are accomplishing the task. Or they may be so unfamiliar with the whole process that they cannot make intelli-gent suggestions. Regardless of which process is used, though, the end product should be kept in mind. Will this job—performed in the manner prescribed in the task analysis—produce the results we want in the best possible manner? If we keep this goal in mind, we should be satisfied that we have a usable task analysis.

JOB DESCRIPTION

We won't say much about the job description, except to point out that we have to be careful in developing training programs around things that people *don't* do on the job. The task analysis tells us the steps to be taken to do the job, and it's bad when we get into a class and hear the employees (students) say, "But that's not the way we do it on the job." To prevent such things from happening is why we do a task analysis in the first place. For the same reason, we need to make sure that the job description includes the activity we're training on. It is much worse when we hear the students say, "We don't even do that job anymore."

There is, however, something about the job description we should note. Sometimes, in an effort to be all inclusive and not miss anything that we might want an employee to do, we add a phrase at the bottom of the job description that goes like, ". . . and such other duties as may be assigned." This may serve the supervisor well at some time, but as far as the trainer is concerned it is a very unfortunate expression. When the trainer is trying to develop a program to bring employees up to standard then finds that the supervisor has the right to assign other activities for which there are no written standards and no task analysis, he or she has no choice but to let that employee go untrained as far as formal training is concerned.

Incidentally, it isn't the trainer's job to see that task analyses exist for every job, and it is certainly not the trainer's job to prepare them if they do not exist. Neither is writing or overseeing the writing of job descriptions a training function. When someone takes on the job of becoming an instructor in an organization, it is not a license either to remake the organization with regard to standards, job function or assignment, or to do a task analysis to show that the job is being done improperly. Best put, "The job description of someone in the training function isn't to see that the everyday job is described well and analyzed properly, or that there are measurable standards for those jobs."

JOB STANDARDS

Let's close this unit with a look at the importance of having standards for the jobs we're training people to do. We've already seen that it isn't the trainer's job to write the standards or to see that they are written, but it is the trainer's concern if they do not exist. It isn't likely that we can ever train anyone up to a satisfactory standard if no standard exists. As we'll see in the next chapter, we write our training objectives based on the job standards so we can let the trainees know what we expect of them at the end of the training program. We will also find in the chapter on Evaluation that we measure our training successes by seeing if the trainees can meet the standards of the job when they get back home. If no standard exists, we cannot get started because we have no real, measurable goal; and if we don't know where we are going, we certainly won't be able to tell when we've gotten there.

As we might guess, writing standards isn't the easiest thing we will ever be called upon to do. We've already said that the trainer shouldn't be the one to write these standards, but he or she can look pretty silly going to a training situation to train someone when there's no standard that tells when the job has been done well. It's sort of like playing a competitive game without knowing the rules until the game is over. It doesn't make much sense to start off on a trip somewhere without knowing much more than the general direction of the place we want to go. Just because standards are hard to come by doesn't mean that we give up trying to get them. The truth is, somebody, somewhere has a standard for every job. If nothing else, we simply ask any supervisor how a person is doing and he or she will tell us immediately. This means that there is a standard by which to measure the job. The supervisor can even tell us how one employee rates against another, meaning that the standard is already in use. It may exist only in the supervisor's head, but it's there, nevertheless.

There are some basic rules for a good standard, and in the next chapter we'll see the importance of this. The job standard should be one that is measurable, observable, and certainly attainable. A job standard isn't some kind of impossible dream or pot of gold at the end of a mythical rainbow. It is a real set of behaviors that can be attained all the time by qualified workers.

It is stated in such a way that it can be understood and observed by anyone familiar with the job, and can be observed in the same way by different people looking at various people doing the same job. For example, if we want somebody to do a job within two hours with a maximum of five errors, anyone who knows the job and comes along to do the measuring and observing can tell if this job is being done up to the stated standard.

Some standards are easier to state than others; but if we expect to appraise a job, we ought to be able to tell the person doing it what is expected in the same measurable terms we plan to use in the appraisal. If our appraisal is going to be very general ("employee should do a good job"), we won't have a very measurable standard; and since we don't know what a good job is, we won't have a very good training program either.

For example, if the job involves customer contact, we could have the standard that the employee should get along with customers. There are some things we can teach to help get along with customers, but it will be difficult to measure our success in specific terms if that's all we have for a standard. We could measure the job by the things that make up good customer-contact activity. We could measure it in terms of number of complaints or, if we're putting someone new on the job, in terms of the reduction in number of complaints.

It could be stated, "The employee will receive no more than two written complaints during any quarter." We could put it on a reducing basis, "The employee will receive ten percent less complaints each month during the first six months on the new job with no more than ten in any month." Or we could go strictly positive with, "The customers will express themselves in a favorable way towards the organization (or department) in some overt way at least three times a month collectively." This may sound of little value, but the trainer knows the things that bring favorable comments and the things that bring overt, unfavorable comments.

Another way of dealing with this standard on customer contact is to deal with those things which we consider good actions when dealing with customers. We could say that during the dealings the employee will always offer assistance to the customer, will offer at least one other product for sale before the final sale is concluded, or will make known at least two other services offered by this organization. Each of these is a measurable standard and is certainly observable.

The truth is, on the job most supervisors measure such a job on the basis of tonal quality of the voice or on statements made or not made to the customer. We can measure that with a little thought and imagination. If we say that the person is to have a "pleasant voice," it can be pleasant only by somebody's standard; so we say that it will be judged "pleasant" by those who are responsible for approving such things. Or we can say it will be judged equal or better than an acceptable tape by those picked to evaluate such performances. To do this we have tapes of someone saying things that we want said in the way we want them said; then we record the employee to see if the quality matches what we have set as the standard.

For skills jobs the task is much easier. We specify an action and tell how well that action is to be done. We can put the emphasis on time, quality, errors, numbers . . . any one or all of these. We can say that the employee who is doing the job adequately will produce 95 acceptable (saleable) units an hour with no more than five rejects. We can say that the employee will type 95 words per minute with a maximum of three errors, or we can say that the requirement will be 60 words per minute with no visible corrections.

Again, we are stating what the supervisors of these people will accept as *standard* (acceptable) performance. If the supervisors can't tell us what is acceptable, then there is no standard. If there is no standard, then we can't measure the job. If we can't measure the job, then we can't train to a standard. We can't measure the training and probably shouldn't do the training!

WHAT DOES THIS MEAN TO THE TRAINER?

At this stage, one may be inclined to say, "So what?" Why make all this effort? From what has been said, the conclusion should be drawn that the reason for making the analysis is to enable the person *doing the training* to be sure that everything done is pertinent to the job. The trainer himself doesn't have to be the one to do the task analysis. But the trainer should be the one to see that an analysis is available. The instructors will need to know that the training program in which they are participating is based on a sound task analysis. If they have any doubt, they can probably answer this by looking at the behavioral objectives that have been written for the course (or the particular part they are teaching). If they describe the end result in a way that is measurable in terms of each step of the job operation, then they can suspect that someone took a close look at the job. It probably means that some kind of task analysis has been done. If so, then the training is on a sound footing; if not, then there are going to be some problems before the program is over!

Exercises and Questions

1. (This should be an advance assignment for each person reading this chapter.) Notice the step-by-step operation of a waitress in a restaurant as she takes orders, records them, relays them to the kitchen, picks up the food and serves it, and finally bills the customer. Make a flowchart of the operations and see whether it could be simplified. Now make a task analysis of the job as it *should* be done.

2. Dividing the class into small subgroups, pick out a simple job such as that of a mail clerk, service station attendant, or cashier at a supermarket and do a task analysis of the way it should be carried out. Discuss how you would approach a training program on this task. How would you know whether the training was successful? Report to the entire group.

3. Dividing the class into subgroups, pick the job of one of the group members and analyze a portion of it. First, try to pick the specific objectives of the job, then look at how it's *now being done.* After everyone is familiar with the job, do a task analysis, trying to *improve* the operation. (This assignment is lengthy and may need to be done outside the class.)

4. Questions for discussion. How many people in the class have job descriptions for the work they do? What is the difference between a job description and a task analysis? How many people in the group have done a task analysis on their own jobs?

chapter 7
STUDENT
OBJECTIVES

The most important single consideration in the teaching-learning process is the setting of objectives. Taken in proper perspective, the entire course, from beginning to end, should revolve around objectives.

These statements are not intended to be startling. Indeed they should be readily accepted by any instructor who is trying to produce a specific quantity and quality of learning. The statements hold true, however, only if the objectives are realistic and are stated in terms of the student's behavior.

OBJECTIVES: BROAD IN SCOPE, SPECIFIC IN MEANING

We saw earlier that courses should be developed because there is a need, because someone lacks a certain skill or is doing a job wrong. In setting objectives properly, the instructor needs to know what tasks are to be performed, that is, *what the employee is expected to do back on the job.* The instructor needs to know how much of this activity the trainee is to learn in the classroom. Thus the objectives cannot be written, until what is to be learned in organized training is *specifically* known.

But what will be expected of the employee who reaches the door of the classroom the first day? The objectives cannot be written until this too can be stated in *specific* terms.

Finally, the objectives must also state what the employee will be able to do when class is over. First, then, is the narrowing down, next the establishment of "initial behavior," that is, what the trainee can do now, and finally the statement of "terminal behavior," or what the trainee can do on completion of the course. *These things do not come easily.* Courses can be run, instructors can teach, and trainees can come and go without any of these steps having been taken. There is a good chance, however, that *the amount of learning taking place* will be less than what is desired.

The objectives must be stated in meaningful terms, and the instructor should keep them continually in mind while teaching. The tendency is to state objectives in broad, loose terms which are all-inclusive but not specific enough to teach from. Courses in which the objectives are "to teach an understanding," or "to give an appreciation," give the instructor too much leeway. They also fail to state a definite end result. The instructor can never say when the objective has been reached.

OBJECTIVES: DIFFERENT KINDS

Objectives are made up of different components, and in writing objectives three main areas should be covered:

1. There should be a description of the terminal skills (specific actions) the trainee should be expected to perform correctly. These motor skills can easily be described, especially if they are already being done by some people back on the job.

2. The knowledge levels or mental abilities to be attained should be specified. These include facts and specific knowledge areas. These are difficult to express, but should be written out just the same, and accepted by both the instructor and the trainee.

3. Some objectives will specify that ideas, principles, theories, and/or concepts should be understood. This is the trouble spot in writing objectives, because of the difficulty of putting concepts into words.

To illustrate item 3, let us take for example an objective which states that we want to "teach an understanding of the Smith Report." Each of us may believe we know exactly what this means, but probably no two people would be thinking of the same thing. For instance, to the clerk who is responsible for filling out the Smith Report (using figures supplied from whatever mysterious source), "understanding" may simply mean getting the figures in the right rows and columns. It may even include knowing how to perform arithmetic operations with the figures, but it probably would not include evaluating the results.

But what about the supervisor whose decisions are based on the results shown in the Smith Report? To this supervisor, a course which taught an "understanding" of the Smith Report would have to include background information, an explanation of why the rows and columns include the facts they do, and how the results affect the day-to-day job decisions.

It is obvious that objectives would be different for clerks and for the supervisors. In terms of behavior, a course for the clerks would need an objective which describes the clerk's job. For example, it might read ". . . given a set of figures in standard form, the employee should be able to place the figures in the proper rows and columns on the Smith Report so that a grand total can be obtained at the bottom of the page." For the supervisor, however, the objective might read ". . . be able to prepare a detailed analysis of the Smith Report '

OBJECTIVES AND ATTITUDES

What about attitudes? Do we write objectives that cover these? It is often said that just getting all the people together from different work locations is worth the time and money, even if nothing is learned. Such statements are ridiculous *unless the objectives specify something to be learned as a result of this association.* Not many instructors would be willing to list their objectives as, ". . . the trainee should be able to list the problems encountered by the other trainees back on their jobs . . ." Yet, if this is one of the main benefits, it should be so stated. In reality, stating the "association benefit" is often a cover for less-than-adequate learning opportunities in the classroom. This is not to say that there are no benefits to be derived as a result of bringing together people from different departments or different geographical areas; certainly it is a healthy experience. But if this is the main thing to be gained *it should be stated in the objectives.*

MEASURING OBJECTIVES

The preparation of objectives is important, but the measurement of them is even more critical. If the objectives do not allow for their own measurement, they are not good objectives. Let's look at an example.

Take a course in *Problem Solving.* The objective reads, "to teach an understanding of problem-solving techniques." In the course the employees learn (and can feed back) the various steps of getting ideas, testing ideas, making decisions, etc. At the end of the course, the students can list these steps, explain what each means, and describe the dangers of omitting any one of the steps. *But back on the job they cannot solve problems any better than they could before they went to the class.* What is the trouble? Properly stated objectives for this class would have cleared up the matter. A better objective for this course should have been, "The employees will be able to list and explain each *step* in problem solving."

But what if we want the employees to *solve problems better?* Then we must list this in the objective, which might then read, "Given a set of facts, alternate conditions, and a measure of what are acceptable conclusions, the employee should be able to make judgment decisions which are economically (or socially or

structurally, etc.) sound." The definition of "sound" will have to be made clear, of course.

How do we measure objectives? The same way we measure a quart of water or a pound of nails. We set a standard and measure the results against that standard. We specify what the desired "terminal behavior" is to be, then when the course is over, match the learner's *actual* terminal behavior against the *desired* behavior. Are they the same? If so, then we have met our objectives. If not, then the training fell short. But remember that measuring objectives may be as hard as writing them originally. Let's look at another example.

Suppose we have salespeople who are pushing only one line of products, although other lines are more profitable. We may say we will give them a course in selling all items. Without objectives, the course may look like any sales course. But with objectives comes a "task analysis," which means that we must first determine what a satisfactory job really is. It may appear that "selling an even distribution of all lines" is the desired objective. This would indicate a course in selling each product. Suppose, though, that after the course the salespeople still sell only the one line—what then? The objective has not been met; the *actual* terminal behavior is not the *desired* behavior.

If the objectives said only an "even distribution of selling," they were not adequate. We failed to specify the "initial behavior." Do the salespeople really know what all the lines will do? Do they have more competition in some lines than others? Is one line wrapped "prettier" than the others? Is one line an old favorite, well proved, durable, etc.? The task analysis should show this, and other things as well. It may prove that no course is necessary. It may prove that some products will never sell as well as others because of existing conditions. It may prove that the salespeople just aren't familiar with certain products, and that short fact-giving sessions will solve the problem.

Whatever comes out, the final behavior should match the specified objectives. The measurement may be done at the end of the course or back on the job. It may be a simple test in which the trainee can answer an acceptable number of questions or it may be the result of months of observation back at the job site. If the objectives deal with attitudes, there should be a specified way to measure these attitudes. If the objectives deal with concepts or principles, some way should be set up to see if the concepts or principles are being used.

GOOD OBJECTIVES COME HARD

All the effort put into objectives will pay off in good learning if the instructor pays proper heed to them. Historically, objectives have been written as a necessary evil, and not many people (including the instructor) paid much attention to them. Now it is recognized that the course may stand or fall on good objectives. *But objectives come hard.* Often, in an eagerness to plunge right into course preparation, the instructor may lack the patience to determine specific, behavioral objectives. The argument goes like this:

"But why write anything so specific until I get the course content organized?"

"How can you organize the course if you don't know what you want the students to be able to do?"

"I do know!"

"What?"

"I want them to learn about the framus machine."

"What do you want them to know?"

"Everything!"

"Everything?"

"Sure."

"How to build one?"

"Well, no, of course not. But it wouldn't hurt them to know how one is made."

"Why?"

"Because their workers are working on framuses all day, and it would build up the supervisor's prestige to be able to tell how the framus is put together."

"Oh, so the objective of the course is to have the supervisors stand in higher prestige with their workers?"

"No, not really. Their prestige isn't too bad. I just meant it would be nice for them to know about the framus."

"Why are you having this course, anyway?"

"Well, all the other supervisors have had a course except the framus workers. They've been asking for a course, too."

"So the objective is for them to be able to say they've had a course?"

"No, but it would help morale, I expect."

"So the objective is to raise the supervisors' morale . . . ?"

And so on. Left alone, the instructor may well have included the pieceparts of the framus, how to put one together, and probably the step-by-step process of operating it. Why? No real reason, we've just always had a course in framuses.

CONCLUSION

What have we said? Objectives are the most important consideration in the teaching-learning process, because when properly defined they encompass the task, the instructor, the student, the course content, and the back-on-the-job performance. They should be written in terms of behavior, the performance expected of the trainee. If the instructor cannot say what the trainees should be able to do at the end of the course, he or she cannot adequately teach them. Objectives should provide for their own measurement, whether the measuring is done immediately on completion of the course or months later on the job. If attitudes are to be learned, or principles, or concepts, or skills, they should be described accurately in the objectives. It is not easy to write realistic objectives, but then neither is it easy to say for sure what the students will learn in the class. And the two should be synonymous.

Exercises and Questions

1. Properly written objectives should not only specify the behavior (or performance) expected of the student at the end of the learning experience, but also the *conditions* under which the performance is to take place. Dividing the class into subgroups of three or four people, write an objective for someone going through the experience you are now engaged in.

Let each subgroup report (and defend) its results to the entire class.

2. Working in the same subgroups as in Question 1, pick one subject that someone in the subgroup might teach and write an objective for what the students should be able to do at the end of the course. Again, report (and defend) the results to the entire group. *Note*: Be sure the *conditions* as well as the action expected are clearly stated.

3. After each subgroup has reported, all subgroups should get together and determine *how the objective will be measured*. Their findings should be reported to—and discussed by—the entire class.

4. By group activity, arrive at an objective for an indoctrination course for new college hired people. Be sure to include the conditions, expected behavior, and how the results will be measured.

5. With the class in subgroups, write an objective for a program on sales training for newly appointed sales trainees. Report and defend the results, again stating how the results will be measured.

chapter 8
STUDENT MOTIVATION

We have already discussed the various reasons why employees take courses. Whatever the reason might be, though, *we must assume that they would rather learn than not.* But because each employee is different, has a different experience level, and looks for something different from the course, we will find that each has a different amount of motivation. (For our use, we will define motivation as the degree of desire to learn, study, cooperate, etc.)

LEARNING MOTIVATES LEARNING

Since students would rather learn than not, one obvious motivation is the *act of learning.* As students realize they are learning, they are pleased, and are motivated to repeat the process that pleased them. There is a limit to this, however, because learning that comes hard, with many frustrations along the way, may produce satisfaction without much motivation to repeat the process. The kind of learning that best motivates is the "hit and run" type, in which the conditions are just right: the student is highly curious about the subject, the instructor is handling the situation well, and the surroundings are conducive to learning. In such a situation, the training proceeds smoothly, the student grasps the desired information (or skill, concept, etc.), and it is a satisfying experience all around. The student is willing to try again, in fact may want very much to try again. But a long, tiring session, filled with concentration, mental strain, and downright "hard digging" isn't likely to motivate immediately. With some rest and reflection, the student may pick up the desire again, but at the conclusion of the session (whether a day, a week, or longer) the student may just want to wait awhile.

SOME ARE MOTIVATED BY CHALLENGE

Of course, some students find challenge and difficulty their biggest motivations. They warm up to a hard session, and actually look forward to the arduous activity. Generally, these are trainees who have much confidence in their ability and who have come through many hard sessions before. Also, they may be above average in intelligence.

To be a motivating challenge, the classwork (and nightwork, if any) should, as a rule, be the proverbial "carrot-on-a-stick" type. *Except, perhaps, that trainees should get a good chunk of carrot occasionally.* If something measurable isn't going into their minds or becoming a part of their manual skills, they will begin to lose interest, hence will no longer be motivated to learn.

INTEREST AND MOTIVATION

It should go without saying, perhaps, that the learner who loses interest is no longer a learner. Why should he or she be? What motivation is there for one who is confronted with material that apparently is unrelated to his or her job or future? "But wait," someone says. "Don't you know that the material covered is of vital importance to your future?" There is always a good chance that the learner may *not* know these things simply because *nobody has told him or her,* neither the supervisor nor the instructor. Oh, they may have said, "You're taking this course because it's very important to you and to the company that you understand these things." But if, after the course gets going, nothing about it seems to relate to anything in the foreseeable future, the trainee's interest will surely falter.

So the supervisors *and* the instructors have responsibilities to the employees to see that the *application* of the course content is clear. The instructors are limited in their ability to control what the supervisors say about the course, but they have full control over what they themselves say about the importance of the course material to the trainees, its use and place in their future.

In the previous chapter we talked about objectives. If the objectives are clearly stated, trainees should know what is expected of them at the end of the course. They will know only what they are supposed to have the ability to do, though, not what they are expected to do with this ability. Good objectives may make it clear enough, but the instructor should make every effort to be sure that the trainees know what all of this means to them.

Adult students are more interested in the "here and now," the immediate use of learned information, than they are in that which may be of some help in the dim, distant future. They are motivated to learn when they can identify with a problem and believe in the solution. Their interest is aroused when they see that the course material indeed is pertinent to them and their job. The instructor can capitalize on this motivation by continually relating to real life situations. The examples used, the problems solved, the situations analyzed should all be drawn from reality. Examples that are hypothetical, obviously unreal, will not motivate for very long. Even though a certain amount of theoretical material must be included, it should always relate to real life. Many well-designed, well-taught courses have fallen apart because the students just didn't understand how they were to use the information, or how they would benefit from knowing it.

STUDENT VERSUS ORGANIZATION NEEDS

In a way, there is a paradox in looking at why we train and why students learn. If we make a list of reasons why we spend training dollars, it comes out like this:

Save money	Increase efficiency
Increase profits	Prevent accidents
Offer more services	Backfill for vacancies
Meet regulations	Improve quality
Keep up with competition	

On the other hand, if we ask for a list of reasons why trainees bother to take courses, it is different from the above list. As we've already shown, adults live in the here-and-now world,

and need to see something in it for them—*now*. The list therefore looks like this:

Make more money	Self-satisfaction
To keep job	Make job easier
A chance to advance	To keep up with others
Curiosity	To acquire recognition
Peer pressure	

If we look carefully at these lists we see that they are quite different, and there is a different orientation to them. The first one
aims at advantages for the organization. It is totally selfish—in a
legitimate way—in favor of the organization's needs. Even when
it favors the individual, it still has a motive aimed at meeting an
organizational need. "Backfill for vacancies" is great for the
trainees, but the motive for it is to prevent the operation from
suffering when there is a vacancy. Things will run smoothly
during the transition from the outgoing to incoming employee.
"Increase efficiency" actually means getting more work out of
the employees for no more money, or with no more employees.
It is definitely *organizationally* oriented.

Is this wrong? Is this apparent selfishness aimed at destroying
the students or the employees? Should the orientation be different? No, not at all. It's the only way to justify spending the organization's money. There are few places where there is enough
money to run training programs just to satisfy the curiosity of
the employees, but for no gain to the organization. Well, how
about the employees? Are they wrong when they learn only
when they see something in it for themselves? Should they be
concerned only with the organization's needs, regardless of how
it affects them or their lives? Should they get excited about the
prospects of working harder, producing more, with less or the
same money? No. Are they, too, just being selfish? No, again.
They are just being natural. We wouldn't want them any different, really, because as they now are, we can understand their
motivation. If they were totally devoted to the organization's
needs, we'd have trouble understanding them.

How do we make these differences work out to the mutual
benefit of all concerned? Can it be done? Yes. We can be sure
that when we're explaining to the students why we're conduct-
ing this particular course, we avoid listing *only* those reasons for

training that show the organization's interests and orientation. Just to say that "the organization had too many accidents last year, so we're having a safety training program," doesn't do much for those trainees who didn't have accidents last year. Even if we say that the government is cracking down on some of our unsafe practices, we don't do much to motivate the employees. We're going to have to provide motivation by using things from the list of reasons why people learn mentioned earlier. It may be the "recognition" angle, or the competition approach, allowing them to "keep up with others."

Ideally, of course, we should be building team spirit along the way so that the trainees' list and the organization's list look more alike. Actually, as people are in the organization longer, and especially as they rise to levels of more responsibility, we find that the two lists begin to get closer together. Supervisors worry about increasing efficiency; managers worry about competition. They worry about these things because they can see a more direct relationship between what's good for the organization and what's good for them, and, to a certain extent, vice versa. New employees don't have that kind of insight, hourly workers find it hard to bring the two lists closer together, and old-line, hardened employees don't want to bring them together. Of course, some employees at all levels and with different levels of experience and goals will be able to merge their motivation with that of the organization.

The point of all this is that we have to justify the training to those people in management who handle the money, because they must make decisions where to allocate the money that's available. They are more likely to put it where it *obviously* has organizational payoff. But if we want to motivate students, we're going to have to let them see that there is some profit for them. This doesn't say that no learning will take place if they don't see the personal payoff. It does say that there will be more motivation to learn if the reasons given by the instructor for learning are reasons that meet their own immediate goals.

THE UNMOTIVATED

What happens when an employee apparently has no desire to learn? What can the instructor do? The stock answer may be,

"Find out why he or she isn't interested in learning and try to motivate him or her." In reality, such an answer doesn't help the industrial teacher very much. In the short time instructors usually have with the employees, they can't study the problem in depth; they need some approaches they can try in a hurry. There are several things they can do that may help them find out what the problem is, or at least get the student interested in learning. (The instructor may actually be able to motivate the trainee *without* finding out what the problem is.)

One of the first things the instructor should find out is whether the employee is qualified to attend the course, that is, whether he or she is capable of handling the material. A quick check of the employee's education, experience (and past performance, if the information is available) may reveal something of value. If there was an advanced assignment, did the employee do it, and do it right? If possible, the instructor should find out whether the employee actually did the work alone or was coached by someone else.

Suppose the instructor decides the employee should be able to do the work but apparently lacks the motivation to apply himself. What should the instructor do then? Her first inclination may be to let the trainee alone. After all, it's his future and if he isn't interested enough to apply himself, it's his tough luck. While this may be a quasi-acceptable solution in an institution of higher learning, where the student is supposedly on his own, it cannot suffice in an industrial training situation. The *company* has some stake in the matter, and stands to lose when the employee does not learn. There is the matter of lost production time, salary, and expenses during training, all of which will be wasted if the trainee fails to reach the prescribed objectives. So we can't just ignore the problem.

Can the instructor motivate, then? In many cases, yes. Let's assume we cannot determine anything other than the fact that the trainee apparently has the ability to learn but no desire to do so. The instructor may have to be satisfied with treating the symptoms instead of the cause, but if it helps, that's all right. Someone else, back on the job, will have to treat the causes.

What are the symptoms? Is the trainee openly rebellious? If so, the instructor (who must remain in control) must take firm action for the good of the rest of the group. To avoid unnecessary tensions, such a step is best taken at break time (or at lunch or after class). The instructor should present his views firmly but courteously: "Charlie, it seems to me you aren't satisfied with this course. Frankly, we're not satisfied with your part. Is there some problem here?" An approach like this will get things out in the open. The simplest and most effective way to treat the problem is to meet it head-on as soon as possible. Avoid argument, but answer questions. Be honest, but don't make excuses. Remain in control and never go on the defensive. Try to determine, as nearly as possible, what the real problem is. He may say "This material is a waste of time," when he really means that he doesn't see where it will help him personally. He may say "The material should be covered in one week instead of two," when he actually means that he doesn't like being away from his family (or job, or golf, or fishing) for more than one week at a time. Of course, confrontations like this are very rare, but the instructor should be prepared for them when they arise.

The more common situation is the employee who just doesn't do much of anything. You may be convinced that with a little more effort, she would make a good showing and even be of assistance to the rest of the group. *So why not use her to help out?* If you suspect she is bored or not motivated for some reason, but has some useful experiences she could be sharing, call on her to tell the class how she would solve the problem. The information should be pertinent, of course, and something you feel sure she can talk about. Few of us can resist the chance to tell of our past experiences, and here you are giving her the added incentive of staying "in good" with the group. Never be condescending toward this student. Behave naturally, and show that you expect her to be as much a part of the group as anyone else.

If you know that some particular thing you are teaching is important back on the job, there is always the opportunity to motivate the group by making them *show you* how it could be valuable. For instance, you might say "I wonder why they always include this material in this course. Do you people actually use this stuff back home?" Usually they will rise to the occasion and show you what they do with it. In this case they're presenting your arguments for you.

LEAVE THEM ALONE?

There are times in the instructor's life when he must let some
trainees fall by the wayside. It shouldn't happen often, nor to
many trainees, but it does happen on occasion. A good instructor wants every student to pass, or make good, but for the benefit of those who want to succeed, the instructor may finally
have to let an employee remain unmotivated. Instructors who
really enjoy teaching are always uneasy when one of their students is not part of the group, but it's not fair to the company
or to the rest of the class to devote all of the time to one trainee.
Worrying over students who are not taking full advantage of
their opportunities may be some kind of a test of a good instructor. The one who feels this concern has at least one of the
qualities of a good teacher; one who lacks this feeling still has
much to learn about the art of teaching! The instructor will have
to deal with two other problems in the area of motivation: The
under-motivated class and the *over-motivated* student.

THE UNDER-MOTIVATED CLASS

The under-motivated group is easy to detect, but its cause is
difficult to diagnose. It may be that one or two strong individuals in the group are keeping the pace down. It may be that the
group, by unspoken consensus, has just decided not to bear
down. It may be that some psychological block has developed,
and the group members have gotten the idea that they really
can't do any better. Whatever the problem, the instructor should
try to combat it. How? There are several ways, and he or she
may think of others on the spot.

One way to get the students moving is to test them. (This
will be dealt with in more detail in the chapter on testing.) Some
people, for one reason or another, are reluctant to admit that
testing motivates adult students. In reality, tests are one of the
handiest tools the industrial teacher has, not just for motivation,
but for feedback on student accomplishment. If the trainees
know they are going to be tested, they pay more attention and
learn more. They don't do this for fear of what will happen if
they make a low grade, nor do they worry as much about how

they stand in the group. (They care, but they don't mind not being on top.) Their greatest motivation seems to be their own ego. Adults just like to do well, and even though no one but the instructor will see the grades, they try to do well on tests. The instructor can take advantage of this, but will lose the advantage *if it is overdone.* Tests scheduled at logical times in the course will give the students something to shoot at. The instructor may even use this to wake up the lagging class. Casual statements such as, "If past classes are any indication, you shouldn't have too much trouble with the test tomorrow," motivate the class to study hard to compete with other groups (presumably of the same caliber as this one).

Another approach is to chide them along the way by indicating they are not doing as well as others before them. The instructor may observe that, "Perhaps the material is a little too hard for this group," since they don't seem to be moving along well enough. If they are not learning the material and its possible to have extra sessions, this is effective occasionally. If they have to give up their own time, they may start to make better use of the regular time. Instructors have to be the judge of what is best under the circumstances. They should also have the freedom to act when such situations arise. If they are encumbered with restrictions and regulations, they may be so handicapped that they cannot do the things that will produce the most learning.

Positive Reinforcement

When we're talking about motivation, we need always to remember that nothing is more likely to cause a student greater motivation than an action that gave a great deal of satisfaction. When a student does something we like, and we immediately give some kind of recognition, reward, or acknowledgment for it, we call that "positive reinforcement." It's a great tool for motivation, in and out of the classroom. It uses the simple principle that people are more likely to repeat those actions for which they are rewarded, and to avoid those actions for which there is little or no reward, or for which there is actually some perceived punishment

Let's see how it works. We've illustrated it in other chapters, so we'll not dwell on it for long, but all reinforcement takes sometimes is a word of praise or even recognition that the student is in the classroom. When we're trying to get a student to think through a problem, and we recognize that this has just happened—even to a small degree—we do something that shows we know it happened. We don't have to make a big issue of it. We may do no more than remark, "Nice going, Larry. That's using good logic," then pass on to something else.

Reinforcement works in other ways, too. If we're not getting the hoped-for participation from the group, we reinforce any kind of response we possibly can. If a student gives an answer—even if it's wrong—we reinforce the response, if not the answer. "Okay, class, Jill has given us something to work with. Thanks, Jill. Now, do you all agree with this?" We show the excitement over the answer, because it was an answer, not because it was right or wrong. Another way of rewarding response is by coming back to the student's remark later on. We file it away in our minds, then the next time we're on a similar point (or the same one) we say, "You'll remember what Jack said about his experience with this kind of thing. Now, from this we can see. . . ." The fact that we remember it makes it a reinforcement. We can even help with a little body language. When we're talking about a point that has been addressed earlier by one of the students, but one that we feel needs some more reinforcing, we simply turn our heads momentarily, look at the person, pause only slightly, perhaps even nod, then go on with the point we're making. This not only tells the student that we remember—and appreciate—the comment, but also lets the rest of the class see that we remember this kind of contribution.

There's a word of caution that should be put in here about reinforcement, by the way. If we reinforce a student for participating, we should be ready to have that student continue the participation. It's possible that we may build a small monster in the process of getting discussion started. Also, on the other hand, we may do some reinforcing when we don't even intend to. If we have a student who continues to speak when others need to be talking, or continues to relate stories about how it used to be, and we don't need those stories anymore, it's easy to reinforce by nodding and commenting "that's interesting," not realizing we're actually using one of our motivation techniques. We may wonder why that student doesn't stop talking, when we're the one who is causing the talk. How do we avoid this, if we don't want to address the problem directly by speaking to the overzealous student? We simply stop the reinforcing. We don't nod, we don't acknowledge, we don't deal with the information. We remain polite, listen, even look at the person, but that's all. When the person stops, instead of reacting, we go on with what we were saying. We aren't grumpy, we don't frown, *we just don't do anything*!

THE OVER-MOTIVATED STUDENT

It hardly seems that over-motivation should be a problem, and it rarely is, but sometimes employees will get keyed up to the point where they become overly concerned about their progress. If they find anything in class or in the textbook they do not understand, it bothers them so much that it becomes a problem. It may cause a trainee to study later than she should at night, giving up sleep to do so, with the result that she cannot concentrate the next day. She may begin to worry about how her showing will affect her job back home, and add this problem to her worry list. She may become a problem for the instructor both in class and out. During class she is likely to ask questions on everything she doesn't understand, even monopolizing the time. She may soon disgust the others (and probably the instructor) with her concern over even the small items. After class she may take up the teacher's time with long discussions intended to assure herself that she really does understand the material.

In such a case the instructor must assure the student that she is doing as well as can be expected. The instructor can point out that there are others who are having some difficulty, too, but who are just doing their best. The trainee should be urged not to let the nightwork keep her from being alert during the day. The tendency of the student to dominate the time with questions can be handled as described in the earlier section on the "dominator." To some extent she can be ignored or asked to wait and see if the solution doesn't come out clear enough. Somewhere along the way, she may have to be told frankly that she is making something bigger than it should be. If she doesn't relax, she may end up doing *worse* instead of better. Again there is the caution: don't let her use up too much time. It's too bad to lose one student, but *it's better to lose one than a whole class*.

Exercises and Questions

1. Discuss the statement: "Learning Motivates Learning." Is learning always pleasant? (Explain your answer.) Are some employees more motivated by learning than others? (Your answer must be defended by an example.)

2. Since employees arrive at the classroom with different degrees of motivation (desire to study, learn, participate, contribute, etc.), this must be taken into account when the instructor starts teaching. Let each person in the class make a list of ways of determining the amount of motivation students have when they come to class. Record these and then see how they work in *this* class on *this* group.

3. Take a secret (anonymous) ballot from each person in the group on why they are in this class *at this time*. ("To learn to teach" is not an acceptable answer. Why did they come at this time? Were they told to come? Did they volunteer? Did they know what the course was all about?) Record the results on the board, then have the group decide whether there are likely to be differences in motivation among the people in *this* course.

4. Discuss ways in which an instructor can overcome the differences in motivation by adding additional motivation.

5. What is the difference between "interest," "motivation," and "involvement?"

chapter 9
INTERESTING THE STUDENT

It is difficult to separate *interest* and *motivation,* since often they work in a cause-and-effect relationship, interest in a subject motivating the trainee, or lack of interest causing him not to be motivated. If we find ways of keeping interest high, we may have solved the problem of motivation.

THE INSTRUCTOR NEEDS INTEREST

Close examination will often show that the students lost interest right *after* the teacher did. It is revealing to read students' critiques and see how often they will mention the attitude of an instructor toward his subject. They will frequently make such comments as "He really was enthusiastic about his subject," or "She acted as though she wished she didn't have to teach the course."

Trainees are quick to detect a lack of interest on the part of the teacher. There is no reason to think the trainee is going to be any *more* enthusiastic (or interested) than the instructor. Yet, time and again, instructors will go before a class and lecture almost incessantly, exhibiting no apparent interest, but expecting the students to receive their lecture with enthusiasm. If we plot interest curves, we can be sure *the students' curve will not be above the instructor's curve,* at least, not for long.

INTEREST SHOULD BUILD UP

The ideal situation is one in which the trainees arrive in the classroom with a reasonable degree of interest, which begins to build as new information is revealed. The instructor carefully

plots to arouse curiosity and exhibits an enthusiasm that is catching, all of which ends in a rewarding learning experience for both the students *and* the instructor. In reality, what too often happens is that the students come with some interest and are rewarded with an equal amount of enthusiasm on the part of the teacher. Then the teacher's enthusiasm diminishes, instead of building, and less and less effort is put into holding the interest of the trainees. They soon detect this, and the long hours of "sitting it out" begin. By the time the course is over, both the students and the teacher are relieved to be through, and nobody leaves with any real feeling of reward.

THE INSTRUCTOR IS THE KEY

The instructor, then, has the major responsibility to see that the students have an interest in the subject being taught. It is easy for instructors to pass this responsibility along to the students, but when they do so, they pass on a certain amount of control, because they are admitting they cannot generate interest in the subject on which they are supposedly experts.

There is a story about an instructor who kept complaining to the training director about the poor quality of students coming to the courses. The punch line goes, "All of the trainees are just alike. Five minutes after I get started, they're all asleep. Can't you do something about them?" The point 's clear. The instructor felt no responsibility to the students at all. They were not even *his* students; they belonged to the training director. A wise director might have answered "You put them to sleep—you wake them up!"

The important point is that unless the instructor is willing to make the effort to create interest, there isn't likely to be much. They are *his* trainees, it is *his* classroom, and it is *his* subject matter. And it is *his* job to make the trainees feel that it is *their* class and *their* subject matter. That's a difficult task, but how to do it well is the secret of many an instructor's success. When such an instructor notices that interest is lagging, he examines *himself* rather than the students. When the class looks bored or sleepy, he checks his presentation or the clock, perhaps the room ventilation. He may change his approach, give a short break, or start getting class participation. But he *doesn't* just plod along, figuring he'll be through after a while anyway.

INTEREST AND LEARNING

Why worry about interest? Obviously it is a necessary ingredient in successful teaching. Trainees will be thinking about something or other in which they are interested, so to capture their minds, we must capture their interest. *We cannot assume that they are interested just because they are sitting in the classroom.*

In a way, teaching is a game of skill. Instructors are there to help the student learn. They cannot force learning, only aid it. They can create a good learning situation or a bad one. The skill comes in setting up an environment so conducive to learning that the student can't help but learn. This is done in many ways, one of which is to secure and hold interest. With practiced skill, the successful instructor captures and holds the interest of the students; some of the enthusiasm felt for the subject is communicated to them. As a result, they learn what the instructor has to teach.

ENTHUSIASM IS GENUINE

The enthusiasm talked about here is not necessarily the outgoing, bubbly type. It is the genuine enthusiasm generated by the instructor's sincere interest in seeing that her students get a chance to appreciate a subject she knows and considers important. There's nothing mysterious about it. The enthusiastic instructor gets involved with the subject and with the students, and her enthusiasm is infectious. She may or may not be a good public speaker, but one thing is sure: *she is interested in her students and the subject.* The students will take it from there.

HOLDING INTEREST

Interest on the part of the student is a necessary ingredient for learning, so the instructor must know how to get and *hold* that interest. It is easy to say that interest can be gotten by simply showing the relationship between the material taught and the job situation, but this isn't always the answer. Most courses *are* related to the job, but not all of them hold interest. Humor is effective, but not all of the time can be devoted to jokes. Visual aids are excellent for creating and holding interest, but there are times when visual aids are not possible. Participation is a sure way of holding interest and building enthusiasm, but the trainees cannot all be participating all the time. How, then, do the instructors solve the interest problem? They solve it *by using a combination of all these interest builders.*

The instructor refers to the job in his or her lecture: "How many of you handle this kind of equipment back home?" or, "Do any of you ever run into this problem on your job?" He or she knows they do, but lets them bring it out. Now they are not only relating to a backhome situation, they are participating and are involved. The visual aids can be used the same way. "Who recognizes this picture?" or, "Where would you use this piece of gear?" They identify the picture and are involved. They recognize an assembly line, a piece of gear, a certain circuit, *a real situation,* and several interest factors are being used.

For humor, visual aids may include a cartoon relating to the subject. In an electronics class, one might use a cartoon of an instructor going into great detail on how to turn on a light switch. In a computer school, a cartoon of a computer talking back to the operator might be suitable. Cartoons should not be elaborate—just something to pick up interest. If the instructor is adept at it, he or she can use humor where appropriate, but it should be natural and brief. Off-color stories are funny to some, but may be offensive to others, so it is best to leave this type of humor alone.

CHANGE OF PACE

Perhaps one of the surest ways of keeping interest, aside from continuous participation by the students, is to keep the pace changing during the day. Any kind of routine gets monotonous after a while and a good instructor will find ways of adding variety to the schedule. Check the various items on the agenda and do some planning. When long sessions of talking are required, throw in several five-minute stand-up breaks. Where a long series of visuals are required, have a few brief periods during which the lights are on and the group is looking at the instructor instead of the screen. When the classwork has not been too strenuous, give some work outside of class to prepare for the next day or strengthen the present day's coverage.

When particularly tedious material is coming up, the instructor should set the stage for learning. A coffee break beforehand is a good idea, provided additional short breaks are scheduled periodically during the next hour or so. While the longer break is going on, the classroom should be checked for proper ventilation and temperature. When the session starts, the instructor might have a prepared list of short questions to be asked at intervals during the long presentation. The trainees can either write down the answers or speak out in class. The idea, of course, is to break the monotony when necessary, although if interest holds, the questions can be passed over.

TIMING IS CRITICAL

Timing is always important in holding interest, and that dull movie or slide presentation never fits right after lunch. The period following lunch is critical and should be treated differently from the first period in the morning or the last one before lunch. Activity holds interest, and it's important to plan activity, either by the students or the instructor, for the first period after lunch. This is the time for the instructor to come out from behind the lectern and move around the front of the room. Even short trips part way down the aisle will often help, because it keeps the back-row students from feeling that they are not part of the group. Calling for answers from the class, having the students exchange papers for grading and comments, getting them together in small groups—all this will help get over the "after-lunch drag."

There is another aspect of timing that is just as critical. When a stopping time is published or expected, whether it be break, lunch, or end of the day, the instructor should not go beyond it. The instructor who thinks he can get in "just a few more points before we go" has a lot to learn about classroom psychology. Interest starts to waver when the clock reaches quitting time. This is particularly true at lunch time and at the end of the day. The students may have made arrangements for meals or transportation, and their interest in the subject gives way to their interest in meeting these arrangements. It is an unfortunate situation, too, when instructors have not gauged their time very well, and let the time slip by without adequately covering their assigned material. In an effort to make up for this, they may suddenly unload all of the information at once, leaving the trainees stunned. There is no time for questions, they cannot absorb it all fast enough, and little learning takes place. The instructors may feel they have met their requirements, but most likely the students feel that the instructors have badly shortchanged them.

Exercises and Questions

1. Since it isn't likely that the students will be interested in a subject when the instructor shows little or no interest, it's important that the teachers let their interest show. The interest should be genuine and built around the subject being taught. Have a brainstorming session in which the group is to come up with ways instructors can demonstrate their interest. Take 10 minutes to see how long a list can be compiled. Remember . . no negatives. After the list has been compiled, go over it for practicality.

2. Now make a list of ways instructors can kill the interest the students have in a subject. Determine whether any of these have come up in *this* class

3. Examine the following statements, both by instructors and both dealing with interest.

   a) "I don't know where we get these students. They just don't seem to be interested in the subject."

   b) "I don't know what's wrong. I just can't seem to get their interest."

   There is a shade of difference in what they are saying, but there is a lot of difference in the two attitudes. Each has placed the responsibility somewhere. Where? Which instructor would be the most susceptible to teacher training? Why?

4. Attention spans are usually much shorter than class periods. Describe some ways of adding change of pace to hold attention (interest) longer. Subgroups should come up with an hour's worth of teaching that has a change of pace every 20 minutes. (Pick a specific subject and tell what the teacher *and the student* will be doing in each of the 20-minute segments.)

chapter 10
INVOLVING THE STUDENT

It is impossible to talk about interest and motivation without getting finally to the real heart of the matter—*involvement*. If we want to change the behavior of employees, that is, teach them to do things they are now unable to do, we must get them involved in the change. They must become aware that the things going on around them relate to them and affect them very much. Further, *they must become a part of the activity.* They cannot be merely observers; they must be participants. No matter what the activity is, they need to be involved in it. If they are to learn, it must be *their* class, *their* problem, *their* solution. Making sure that they are involved, however, is the instructor's problem.

WHY INVOLVEMENT?

The class is being conducted because there is a particular thing that the employee cannot do, or is not doing well enough, or is doing wrong. When she goes back to the job, she will be expected to do it right. If she has had only a casual exposure to the right way, she isn't likely to be much better when she gets back on the job. Why? Because she has had no real practice at doing the right thing the right way. She has not had to develop any commitment to the correct procedures. She may not even have had to go through the mental processes of reaching the correct conclusions or concepts. If she hasn't been involved, then someone else has done the thinking and the performing.

On the other hand, if she has become involved in the mental and/or physical activities of the operation, she is now better able to commit herself toward doing and thinking the correct thing. She has engaged herself in practice (mentally or physically) and, perhaps for the *first time*, sees how her job really is supposed to be done.

Another reason for involvement, often overlooked, will be discussed in more detail in the chapter on visual aids. Briefly, it is the matter of competing for time in the thinking process of the students. Their minds are always active, thinking about many things. Even when they are not thinking about the subject at hand—when they are bored and not involved—they are still thinking about *something*. The instructor is, in a real sense, competing for time that is going to be spent in thinking either about the subject or whatever is of more interest to the student. The instructor must devise ways of creating the interest and getting the trainee so involved in the class activity that he has little thought-time to put elsewhere. The more participation (hence involvement) the instructor can get from the student, the more thought-time he has captured. This is why dull, monotonous lectures do not keep the student's attention and fail to produce much learning. The alert instructor will recognize this shortcoming and gauge his or her conduct to include change of pace, involvement, or whatever it takes to keep the student's mind in the classroom.

INVOLVING THE INSTRUCTORS

Strangely enough, one of the biggest problems in education either industrial or academic, is to get *instructors* involved in the training. Just being in the classroom and giving lectures is not enough; instructors should be committed to the learning process. They should have the desire to send the learner away better able to do his job than he was when he came to class. Instructors must know whether their trainees are learning; they must know what techniques to use to help them learn best; they must test, study the feedback they get, and adjust their teaching methods accordingly. They cannot be satisfied just to come into class, remain aloof, make a presentation, and leave.

Of course, instructors may not like what happens after they get involved. The techniques they use, the visual aids, the timing, everything, may be all wrong. Nevertheless, real involvement requires that this be found out *and* that every effort be made to correct the problem. *It should not be up to the trainee to adjust to the whims of instructors;* instructors should be willing to adjust to the learning conditions best suited to the trainee.

How do instructors show involvement? (And the students are the first to know whether or not they are involved.) The *involved* instructors come prepared, notes in order, subject under control, and with their own little "bag of tricks" to get the trainee just as deeply involved as they are. They are aware of their own shortcomings. They realize that they aren't so charming and dynamic that the class automatically hangs on their every word. They will know where the rough spots for the trainees are going to be, and they will take them over these spots carefully. They will figure some way to get interest at the very start, and hold it the rest of the time. When they see interest dragging, they will react with something new or different; perhaps a "pop quiz" or a request for comments from the floor. *Their involvement will always cause them to try to get the students involved.*

INVOLVING THE STUDENTS

It is easier to *suggest* getting involvement than it is to *actually* get it. How does an instructor go about getting students involved in class activity, in the teaching-learning situation? There are a number of ways, and each instructor must find the way that works best.

It has already been said that first the instructor must get involved. The things that get the instructor involved aid in building the students' interest and participation. Students will like the course better if they are a part of it, although they may not volunteer to become involved. Just asking an open question isn't going to immediately draw all the group into a discussion. Very few of the trainees will be willing to answer questions openly at first, even when they are sure of the answers. In Chapter 13 we will discuss some training techniques that prospective instructors can try. They must realize that their goal is not merely involvement for its own sake, but as a means to enable the trainee to better learn and retain specific material. The involvement must be centered around this material. If this were not so, then a discussion on politics or the local football team would suffice as a means of building interest. Participation is a directed thing, then, and must be preplanned to aid learning.

An example will help make the point clear. We often hear that a good speaker should start off with impact to get the audience's attention. This is certainly a good idea, but the instructor should remember that a classroom is not a banquet hall, nor is teaching a class equivalent to giving an after-dinner speech. Public speakers must depend on their *own actions* almost entirely to get and keep interest. The audience will stay with them only on the basis of their "personal magnetism," so to speak.

Not so with classroom instructors. They have a power and opportunity not often afforded the speech maker. They can turn the whole thing back on the "audience" and let them be involved while they do practically nothing. For instance, the instructors can break the class into small groups and let them tackle a difficult problem. They can work on it, solve it, and even present the solution to the entire group. All the instructors have had to do is carefully *guide and control* the events. They can ask the group to write something down, identify a problem, volunteer information on any subject, or even give them the right to disagree if they think the instructor is wrong. In fact, successful instructors will want to use *all* of these techniques to improve learning.

The initial joke or opening story is good only in getting attention the first time. From then on, other methods will have to be included.

The trainees are involved because they have been led to do a thing by the conscious effort of the instructor. It rarely happens by accident; *it usually comes as a result of some kind of force.* Although *force* may sound too harsh, in reality that's what it is. When the instructor says "Pick up your pencils and make a list of the five main steps," involvement is being *forced.* The trainees will not refuse to do it, and they are involved at the instructor's request. So it is with other methods. Even controversy is a means of forcing the students to come out of any lethargy they might feel. Controversial statements, calculated to arouse the students, will force participation.

The instructor may assign some students to explain various points to the rest of the class, either on the spot or after preparation. This means that these students will be on their feet talking, explaining, drawing on the board. They are involved because the *instructor* planned it that way. It should never be forgotten, however, that the students are not expected to be instructors, and any assignment for them to teach should be on a selective and limited basis.

What about more subtle means of getting the group involved? The trouble with most of them is that probably not *all* of the group will respond to the technique used. For instance, a challenging, step-by-step problem-solving exercise in which the group carries the burden of the work is a fine approach for involvement. The procedure is for the instructor to lead the way, with the group responding with obvious answers to questions. They become involved and encouraged with easy questions at first, but as the class progresses, the questions get harder, and the answers more sophisticated. By carefully gauging the steps, the instructor can get *most* of the group through to completion. The result is a satisfying and profitable learning experience for those who went all the way.

The trouble is that some of the group may have dropped off along the way. For these it will be a frustrating and unrewarding exercise. Often there can be no alternative, of course. There is a way to keep from losing some of the trainees who did not complete this exercise. As with any complex sequence, it is important to review each step to help make it clear. On the second explanation, those who missed it the first time will be watching closely, hoping to clear up their trouble.

There is a built-in involvement technique in the above procedure. If the entire process is done on the chalkboard or an easel of some kind, there will be almost constant natural movement by the instructor. It is a natural movement which the students will follow. However, if the operation is done from behind the speaker's stand, this attention-getting part of the exercise will be lost.

MEANINGFUL INVOLVEMENT

We need to put in a note of caution about "forced" involvement. If we have to resort to this method, and we certainly do on occasion, then we ought to be aware that we're having to do it because we're not successful with our regular techniques. We've lost the students and have to resort to more or less of a gimmick to get them back. When this happens, we should ask ourselves, "What happened? How did we lose them? What's wrong with the method of instruction we had planned for this particular section of the training day? Did we misjudge the students' capacity to handle the design? Has this failed before and we weren't alert enough to notice it?" These are serious questions and we need the answers.

A better approach is to determine that we will never have them doing just *busy work*, if we can possibly help it. The students can tell when we're asking them to do something just for the sake of doing it; at least, most of them can. Surely there is plenty that they need to be learning without using up valuable time with meaningless activity, designed to keep them awake, because we couldn't find a learning design that could keep them alert otherwise. When we break them into subgroups, it ought to be because that particular method of instruction is the best one to accomplish the learning we want to happen at that time, because it meets our goals for learning and will get us feedback, because it will allow the students to explore possibilities or come up with alternatives or find solutions.

If we're looking for gimmicks, there are plenty of them around. Some instructors enjoy playing games with students— building in some sensitivity-type activity—then letting the students see what they have just done. The students may even enjoy it, may even learn something from it, but if they aren't learning what we want learned in that time slot, we'll have difficulty justifying our effort and time usage. We don't have to defend our processes, since we've usually agonized over the different approaches we could take, weighed the good and the bad in each against the desired outcome, and settled on a method or process that best suits the group, the facilities, the subject, and our skills. At the same time, we don't want to be put into the position of defending a process that we know doesn't do what we want done. We don't want to have to explain to students that we're using this particular design because the one we had in mind didn't keep them interested.

This doesn't eliminate experimenting, by the way. There's no reason why we can't try out a design and decide even in the middle of it that it's not getting us where we want to go and switch back to one with which we're more comfortable. The easiest way to judge an involvement exercise is to ask ourselves, "Are we using it because we like to do that sort of thing, or do we think this is the right time for this involvement process to be used to meet this learning objective?" As we keep pointing out, the most important person in the classroom is the student; the most important thing that can happen is learning.

INVOLVEMENT TECHNIQUES

So far we have discussed a number of ways to get involvement, and in subsequent chapters others will be discussed. Let's see if we can put together a list of ways the instructors can get involvement and include a little discussion about each. We call the reader's attention to Chapter 14 on Classroom Techniques and especially to the section in that chapter on *Systems of Instruction* and *Teaching Techniques*. These will help the reader understand what we're trying to accomplish as we use the different techniques of instruction.

Technique	Discussion
1. Questions & Answers	This is the most obvious and most often used technique for involvement. It is easy, and anyone can use it on any subject. It can be overworked, and the questions may or may not be relevant.
2. Student-generated Questions	The class can simply be assigned the task of coming up with one question on certain material, or the teacher can ask for volunteers. The students can become the expert, approving or disapproving the answers.

3. Subgroup Activity

This, too, is often used and is highly successful for most people. The activity should be clear in goals and have built in accountability as to who and how the reporting is done.

4. Student Teaching

Assignments are made ahead of time; rules for time and content are given and enforced. The same student can be used more than once, but the technique is more effective if the task is spread around.

5. Group Student Teaching

Subgroups are formed with the task of teaching a certain subject, using two or more members of the subgroup as teachers. Ideally, there is a time limit, and several people present material.

6. Guided Notes

This is an easy way to force some involvement, and it provides a source of feedback at any time. The teacher gives out partial notes, students fill in from class activity.

7. "Pick up your pencils"

Sometimes it's a good idea just to invite the students back to the class world by simply saying, "Pick up your pencils and list . . . " The assignment should be relevant but not time consuming.

8. Reading Assignments

In order to emphasize the importance of the material in a chapter or a manual, we can devote a few minutes of class time to reading, then ask for

9. Debating

key phrases, facts, sentences, or conclusions to be reported individually or from subgroup consensus.

The sides can be drawn quickly by saying, "This side of the room take the Pro, the other side the Con . . . " This gets quick involvement, provides insight into the problems and forces the students to make a commitment.

10. Simulation

Any kind of simulation is good involvement, whether it be role play, case study, action maze, management game, or incident process. Look for real life, but do not go into too much detail.

11. Impromptu Case Study

Without any preparation (apparent), continue a problem being discussed with, "Okay, let's suppose we have a situation where production is down in all the plants, but there are no union problems, maintenance is good and there is little turnover . . . how would you begin analysis on determining the problem? Break into groups . . . "

12. Impromptu Role Play

Casually drop into a role play by saying, "You said you'd call the employee in for a discussion. Let me be the employee . . . what would you say to me? Anybody can enter in."

13. Role Reversal

In any situation, reverse roles. "Let me be the student, teach

> me . . . You be the employee,
> I'll be the boss . . . " "Swap
> sides in the debate and argue
> the other way . . . Tom, swap
> with Sue and you be the union
> steward, Sue the boss . . . "

Certainly there are many more techniques for getting involvement, including many combinations and variations of the ones we've listed here. The ideal thing for the instructors to do is to find things they are comfortable with, things that get a high degree of involvement, then use those while they find additional ways of improving the class participation. There is good reason for finding something we can be comfortable with, so that if we experiment with something that fails, we can quickly fall back on that which is a sure thing and that takes little thought or effort on our part. The hazard is that we will get too comfortable and fail to use our imagination and ingenuity to come up with something especially for the particular group or course we are teaching.

More and more, we're seeing that learners learn more and are generally more interested if they can participate actively in the teaching-learning process. Things like "inter-active video" or "computer-assisted instruction" are really efforts to tie the learner more closely to the learning activity. As processes get more sophisticated and more technical, there is a tendency for instructors to become frightened over learning how to use these new approaches. Of course, the best way to ease that fear is to become familiar with the techniques, but it will also help—and perhaps this is the best approach of all—to recognize that only the technique changes, *not the goal.* The goal is to increase the learning by getting the learners involved in it as quickly, as intently, and as easily as possible. The "inter-active" efforts accomplish this quite well!

This is not to say that an ordinary instructor, in an ordinary setting, without the more exotic techniques available, cannot accomplish the desired involvement and hence the desired learning. Even with such a simple and time-tested method as the lecture, the teacher can use questioning in such a way that the learner starts to think on his or her own; and the resulting involvement produces the necessary thought processes that cause learning. It works like this:

- The teacher gives some information on the data or skill to be learned.
- The teacher asks a question designed to challenge the students to put their "thinking caps" on.
- The students begin to extend the remarks made by the teacher.
- The teacher weighs what is said, accepts or returns it to the class for further refinement. This goes on until the teacher and the students are comfortable, then the next topic-skill is introduced.
- The process repeats itself in the same or modified fashion.

The experienced teacher finds that the above process works over and over and over again, class after class, subject after subject. There is pretty good evidence to show that the *students also get good at it!* They've been in so many classes where this technique is used that they don't have to learn a new way of performing as they would with an action maze or a business game. They already know what to expect from the teacher and what the teacher expects from them. They're comfortable as soon as they realize the teacher will wait them out for an answer and will use their answer in a meaningful way to further *their* learning.

FEEDBACK FROM INVOLVEMENT

In Chapter 14 we will talk about getting and using feedback, but let's notice here that careful attention to the involvement techniques listed above will supply sufficient feedback to allow the teacher to know exactly where the students are at any given time during the instructional effort. It is important of course, that the instructor be aware of the purpose of feedback and know what to do with it when he or she gets it. Simply put, anytime the students participate in an active way, they are to some extent telling us where they are. It is our invitation to read a printout on them. The information may be limited or exten-sive, representing the whole class, a portion of it, or only one individual, but there is data there, and we should practice using it after we've learned how to get it.

The other side of the involvement coin, is a match for the other side of the feedback coin: when we get feedback from the involvement, so do the students! It's their chance to learn something about where they are, and it's up to us to help them understand the data they are getting. It's a shame when they say or do something and don't get back any kind of evaluation as to where they are in the learning process. (That's another reason for them to know what the objectives are. If they know what's expected of them, when they do get this feedback they can match it against where they're supposed to be.) In either case, it's important data. Skilled teachers who get feedback easily, will find out much about the students and, at the same time, will allow the students to find out much about themselves.

VISUAL AIDS CAUSE INVOLVEMENT

As we will see in the next chapter, visual aids draw attention to a *focal point*, and with enough movement (i.e., enough *different* projected pictures, various models, etc.), the trainee's eyes are almost forced to stay at this point. If the visual aids are realistic enough to properly portray job situations or suggest *real* solutions, the trainee will identify easily with what is being shown and said. The trainee will be involved in other words, and will stay this way until the situation becomes unreal or uninteresting.

A final note on involvement: involvement makes the difference between interest and disinterest, between participation and withdrawal, between motivation and boredom. *It is not something the instructor can arbitrarily rule out as not fitting the course.* Much of what is blamed on "mental fatigue" is really just plain *boredom.* Instructors who would rather stand and lecture than bring the students into discussion, or get them to participate, to make it "their class," should ask themselves, "What makes me think I'm so charming?" To that question they should give an honest answer, and if the answer isn't very flattering, they would do much better to use the tried and true methods that come closer to *guaranteeing learning!*

Exercises and Questions

1. Determine by discussion whether the class agrees on the truth or falsehood of the following statement: "If students are involved, they will be interested; if they are interested, they will be motivated to learn; if they are motivated, they will be more likely to learn than if they are not motivated." (Get a group consensus and discuss why and why not.)

2. Now *decide* whether the negative of the statement in Question 1 is true, i.e., "Not involved, then not interested, then not motivated, then not likely to learn." Those agreeing and disagreeing must give examples. Also, they must decide *generally* whether this statement is true or false.

3. With subgroups of four or five, see which can come up with the greatest number of ways of getting involvement. Record this list, then see whether the other subgroups have any suggestions that do not appear on the list. Now the class should decide which of the techniques listed are generally used in the courses with which they are familiar.

4. Looking at the list from Question 3, decide how many techniques that are *not* used could be used without much additional effort. Would it be worthwhile?

5. Discuss the following statement and decide—as a group—whether the class agrees or disagrees: "I don't like all this talk about motivation, involvement, and interest. I just tell them if they don't get the information, it's their own tough luck, and out they'll go. Believe me, I get plenty of involvement."

chapter 11
VISUAL AIDS

So much has been said about visual aids in recent years that it seems impossible that they are not an accepted part of every training program. Unfortunately, only lip service is given to them in many training situations. But it is important to note that not all visual aids are good visual aids. Besides the practical, useful, well-designed aids, there are those which do not meet any criteria for producing learning. *They may, in fact, prevent it.*

WHAT ARE VISUAL AIDS?

Very simply, a visual aid is *anything* used in the classroom that attempts to teach by showing, or by appealing to the sense of sight. It may be a chart, a chalkboard, a demonstration device, a

motion picture, or any one of many different kinds of projected pictures. It may be something held in the hand, or a many-colored, professionally drawn piece of art work that has been photographed and projected on the screen.

Why define visual aids? Because so often they are put into a small category of projected pictures, and either used or rejected. To better understand why it is important to use visuals, we have to think of them in the broadest sense. The supervisor who gets a teaching assignment may try to soothe her conscience by saying that visual aids belong to the "professionals." Since the supervisor is a nonprofessional, she will just limit herself to lecturing. But even she resorts to visual presentations when she gestures or indicates with her hands that a thing is "this shape," or "so high," or points "in this direction." When the instructor makes a mark on the chalkboard or shows a chart on the easel, she has introduced visuals into her teaching.

There should be a clear understanding, of course, that it does not necessarily follow that any visual aid is a good aid just because it fits the definition of a visual aid. Some have felt that a picture, even a bad picture, is always worth a thousand words. So far as bad pictures are concerned, even a *few* good words are often better. So it is as much a failing to use bad pictures in training as it is not to use pictures at all.

WHY USE VISUAL AIDS?

Many studies have been made on the use of visual aids in learning, comparing their use and nonuse in presenting the same material. Obviously visual aids always come out in front. While studies vary, a conservative figure would indicate that at least 75% of what we learn is through the sense of *sight*. In addition, we forget about 75% of what we *hear* after two days.

This means that *practically everthing we say* in the training room is useless unless it is emphasized in some way by visuals. This is discouraging when we think how often training time is taken up with the instructor's talk. Visual aids not only increase learning because of their appeal to the eye, but also because they generate more interest and offer a change of pace.

Visuals are an excellent way to capture the trainee's attention. We use visuals because the eye will follow a moving picture or a changed picture. No matter what is being said or who is saying it, the eye will automatically glance toward movement, thus distracting the mind momentarily. Visuals enable the instructor to take advantage of this phenomenon. When slides or other pictures are projected and changed at frequent intervals, the eye goes directly to the new picture. Of course movies provide continuous movement, but few instructors have enough movies to use them for entire sessions. (Even movies would become ineffective after awhile, though, because of the need for a change of pace.)

EYES MOVE FAST

Instructors often make the mistake of assuming that the eyes of the trainee can only cover as much as can be talked about by the instructor. Instructors will project a detailed picture on the screen, then spend long minutes discussing it in much detail. They will point to each new item as though the trainees are seeing it for the first time. In reality, the eye can cover even the most complex details very rapidly, and the trainees will soon become bored *as they wait for the instructor to catch up.* The instructor has the option of re-doing the visuals so as to show smaller portions of the subject at one time, or the instructor can continue to use the complex one and admit that the students will have covered the material many times (with their eyes) by the time it is discussed.

Is there anything wrong with letting the students see all of the material, even though the instructor isn't ready to talk about it yet? Naturally not, because presumably they already have a complete outline of the subject being discussed. But it is incorrect to call something a "visual aid" which in fact covers much more than is being discussed at any given time. Of course if it is necessary to see where the smaller item being discussed fits in the scheme of things, then by all means the whole picture should be shown.

A better way of doing it, though, is to show the overall picture and indicate the location of the piece or part with subsequent pictures. For example, if it is necessary to discuss a portion of a schematic or part of a complex form, show the whole schematic or form with the smaller portion outlined in color (or set off in some other suitable way), then show the smaller part blown up to cover the entire screen. It's always a good idea to show the whole concept first so the student will know where the small portion fits in. Even though the full schematic or form may be almost unreadable, the student will get the proper perspective, and as smaller parts are enlarged will be able to understand their functions. *Under no circumstances,* of course, should the instructor try to teach from the unreadable visual!

The other alternative is to simply use only one picture, showing the whole drawing or idea, and teach from it. Here the problems increase, because it becomes difficult to hold the students' attention. They will look for a while at the place indicated by the instructor, then their eyes will begin to wander to other places on the screen, and soon their attention will be wandering, too. Interest will pick up when the instructor points to another part of the picture, but there is likely to be a continuous going and coming of interest. It should be mentioned here that even worse than leaving one picture on the screen too long is to show one with several items on it and *never indicate exactly which one is being talked about.* While the students are searching for the subject matter, the words are being lost because the students' attention is directed to finding the right spot on the screen.

The picture that has the entire message on it has another drawback. It is usually too complex to be meaningful. Often the lettering will be so small that it can't be read from the *front* row, much less from the rear of the room. Instructors have been known to refer to their notes while showing a picture because even they couldn't read the copy on the screen! Sometimes only those in the front can make out what is being shown, even though *those in the back row have just as much right to see what's going on.* Passing out copies of the material doesn't solve the problem of unreadable projections either, because then the handout becomes the visual, and the projection on the screen becomes nothing but an obstruction to learning!

We've been talking here about projected visuals, but the same holds true for any kind of device whose purpose is to help the student learn through the use of the eyes. The easel, flannel boards, chalkboards all need to be seen to be understood. The material needs to be simple and concise; it needs to be directly connected with the subject being discussed by the instructor.

MAGNETIC AND FLANNEL BOARDS

More will be said later about the use of the chalkboard, but first we will consider the *magnetic* and *flannel boards*. These help make it easy for an instructor to build up a presentation point-by-point. (Of course, a little ingenuity on the part of the instructor does no harm.) For instance, pictures of products or pieces of equipment (or almost anything else the teacher wants to show) can be cut and placed on the board when needed. As the trainer makes his point, he simply places the item on the board and all the trainees get the point easily. It is possible with some of these boards to use a combination of magnets, chalk, and projected visuals. In addition to being excellent instructional devices, these boards appeal to the trainees just by the sheer "gimmickry" of the procedure. They watch if for no other reason than to see what is going to happen next.

There is a caution here that all instructors should heed: never let the mechanics of using visuals get so interesting that the trainees lose sight of the subject and concentrate on the operation itself. For instance, when a working model is being used to explain a certain subject, the operation of the model should never overshadow the subject itself.

HOW ELABORATE SHOULD VISUALS BE?

The question of how much time should be spent in preparing visuals will always have to be left up to the judgment of the instructor, at least until some way is found to determine the optimum effectiveness of different degrees of "showmanship." No doubt an elaborate visual has more impact than a crude counterpart. The question is, where is the point at which the time, effort, and material involved in producing an outstanding visual are worth more than what the trainees learn from it? So far, all that can be said is that any visual that is readable, to the point, and generally neat is better than no visual at all, and color is more pleasing than black and white. (*It should be meaningful color, and not too harsh.*)

There is one standard to be used in determining how sophisticated a preparation should be, and that is the class itself. How sophisticated are the students? What would appeal to them? A group of top management people would probably expect something better than crude hand-drawn charts projected on the screen in black and white—if time and money would have allowed something better. On the other hand, a group of line craftsmen might be overawed by a "razzle-dazzle" presentation in which all visuals are commercial art, projectors come from concealed cabinets, and the screen appears automatically from the ceiling—unless that is what they are used to in all of their training.

There is another consideration: How many times will the visuals be used? For a one-time presentation, unless the occasion or the subject is extremely critical and demands the best of everything, it may not be economical to spend the time and money in preparing elaborate visuals. If the course will be taught several times, the cost of good visuals becomes only a small part of the overall training cost. The salaries of the instructors and the employees who come off the job for training may well justify spending considerable money to provide adequate visuals. One thing is certain: *Visuals will never be as good as they should be unless they are given proper consideration at all stages of the course preparation.*

CAN VISUALS HINDER LEARNING?

It has already been said that only *good* visuals result in more learning than lecturing does. It is also true that bad visuals may either hinder learning or result in incorrect learning. Visuals that cannot be clearly seen or understood may frustrate the student to the extent that the student stops trying to learn. Visuals that present material in an awkward or complex manner may cause the student to think she understands something when she actually does not.

There are some subtleties in making visuals that may cause the student to misunderstand a subject if they are overlooked. For example, suppose the instructor wants to illustrate the fact that we forget 75% of what we hear after two days. Comparing the "forgetting" with the "remembering," he draws a bar chart showing the 75% on one side and 25% on the other. The larger bar he labels "Forget," and the smaller bar he labels "Remember." This seems to be adequate, but in reality the visual is misleading. The 75% bar is *three times* as long as the 25% bar. Unless there is some labeling clearly expressing "75%," the trainee may subconsciously get the impression of a one-to-three ratio. When asked later to state what he has seen, he may think in terms of $33^1/_3$% and $66^2/_3$%. The instructor would do better to illustrate the above fact with a pie-chart, three-fourths of which is one color, labeled "75%," and the remaining portion of which is another color, labeled "25%." Now the trainee can clearly see the one-fourth, three-fourths relationship. Later, the pie-chart will come to mind, and the student will remember the correct figures. The point is, of course, to make sure that the visual says what it is supposed to say. *If it can be misunderstood, it most likely will be* by some students.

PREPARING VISUAL AIDS

There are a number of things to consider when we start to prepare visual aids, but time will allow us to look at only the more basic considerations. We'll look at some rules which give us an insight into how visual aids can be produced simply but effectively. First, let's look again at the words "Visual Aids." The description says it is an *aid*, not something that will do all the teaching for us. The description also says that what we produce should be of a *visual* nature, at least implying that it should be a picture or visualization of something. Putting it another way, a visual aid is something that aids the student and the teacher in the teaching-learning activity by presenting something that can be *seen*, because seeing it will be a more effective way to learn than hearing, touching, smelling, or tasting it. With this thought in mind we can now look at the basic rules for preparing visuals and understand why we're planning to use them in the first place.

1. Visuals should be horizontal.

Most screens are horizontal, and this allows full use of the screen. It also allows for pro-

2. Material should be proportional to the frame.

jection over the heads of the students.

For maximum size, design the original to make use of all the frame—horizontally designed, horizontally photographed, horizontally projected.

3. Use color for a purpose.

Color should be used, but only because there is a message that can be transmitted better with color. Visuals should teach, not win art contests!

4. Avoid over-illustrating.

Make the visual single-purposed where possible. One message, one visual, is a good rule.

5. Orient the viewer.

Whether with arrows, colors, or words, let the viewer know immediately what to look at and where it is on the screen.

6. Use visuals in moderation.

Limit the visuals not only to the message, but also to the students' endurance time. Go to another format to break up the monotony of too many visuals.

7. Know the purpose of the visual.

In designing or selecting a visual ask, "Why am I using a visual at all?" The answer should tell if the one we pick is the right one.

Perhaps it's worthy of note here that in many organizations the visuals are prepared, if not designed, by people in the graphic arts department of the operation. This means that they are most likely interested in producing a quality product *by their standards.* Their training is not in producing learning, but in producing attractive visuals; and for this reason we may find that though the visual is beautiful, it violates the rules described above. This suggests that we had better not give them just an idea and let them have free rein with color, design, layout, content, etc. They may not understand or even like our idea, especially the simplicity of it, and in order to prepare the visual properly they need a good explanation of its *learning* goals. An even better solution is to have them attend a session of our regular instructor training program that is devoted to how people learn.

WHICH VISUAL AID TO USE?

There seems to be a perpetual argument over which kind of visual aid is best. Some discount the chalkboard, others have no use for overhead projectors, and some belittle the slide projector. What it all amounts to is that *all* kinds of visuals have their place and each has its own strengths and weaknesses.

The best visual to use is the one that will best produce the learning desired within the limitations of the classroom, available equipment, preparation time, and budget. Often the instructor has no choice, because the type of visual to be used has already been determined by the equipment in the classroom. Entire books have been written on the subject of visual aids, and so no effort will be made here to discuss the advantages and disadvantages of every kind of projector and technique. Rather, we will consider some of the more common classroom devices, and what the instructor should hope to accomplish with each.

PROJECTION EQUIPMENT

Motion Pictures

The motion picture, as has already been pointed out, is excellent both as a training tool and attention getter. Supervisors who come to the classroom as teachers are limited to "shelf" films, since they aren't likely to have the budget, time, or experience to make movies just for their use. There are many good films available on a variety of subjects, however, and these should be given careful consideration. Most industries have their own libraries of films which either are made by them, or deal with subjects relating to their activities. This would be a natural place for the instructor to look first.

In addition, most companies also have catalogs of available films, and the instructor may find suitable films that can be borrowed from other industries. Even if a film does not exactly fit in every case, the instructor may still be able to use it, explaining that "certain procedures are obsolete, or are done differently in our company." Unless the film contributes so little that it is a waste of time, the trainees would generally prefer to see it anyway. There are certain operations which almost have to be shown *in motion* to be understood. For this, there is no substitute for a film.

Slide Projection

For compact storage and ease of operation, perhaps nothing is as effective as the slide projector. It also, like motion pictures, allows the use of color. Equipment now available in almost every training location allows for showing large numbers of slides by remote operation. The slides can be sorted, changed, replaced, and substituted in a matter of moments. A presentation can be stored in the same cartridge that is used for projecting, so the instructor has merely to pick out the container for a particular subject, and the visuals are ready to go. Since most projectors change the slides almost instantly, the instructor can even build a sequence easily and effectively, with each slide adding a subsequent step. The instructor can use color to help the buildup, and with remote control at a fingertip, does not have to break the presentation to go to the next slide. The movement attracts the student's interest, and well prepared slides help to hold it. The same remote control may even allow for reversing the slides to return to an earlier one, if there are questions. The teacher can stand up at the front, use a pointer if necessary, and easily keep control of the group.

For all the advantages, slide projection has several drawbacks, and the trainer should be aware of these before using slides.

One disadvantage is the necessity for having the room in almost total darkness. If any extraneous light shines on the screen, much of the color will be lost to the audience. Any time lights are turned off in a classroom, there is the danger of losing some of the students through drowsiness or inattention. This is particularly true if the instructor spends too much time on one slide, as was discussed earlier in this chapter. Where commercial services are used, slides have the disadvantage of being rather expensive, especially for one-time use. Commercial art work is also expensive, especially if the slide is to be on the screen for just a matter of seconds. When these services are available through internal sources, the cost to the company is considerably reduced. Time is also a prime consideration, although most cities now are able to provide one- or two-day service in producing slides.

The problem of light in the classroom can be remedied somewhat by having a light in the rear of the room, or directing a light against the wall or ceiling. This will provide enough light to let the students refer to written material and take notes, if necessary. This may also be of help to teachers, since they may need a source of light to read their own notes.

Filmstrips

Filmstrips, or series of continuous still shots on single rolls of film are also easy to store and use. It's possible to have a roll of over a hundred frames in one small can, making storing and carrying very easy. Since there is no cutting or mounting to be done, the production is quite reasonable, too. Once there is a master negative, reproducing the filmstrips is a simple matter. Laboratories will usually print, box, and label for you at very reasonable rates, and you get a roll of film that's ready to project. The filmstrip projector can be one with automatic advance —triggered by sound messages sent from a tape or record narration—or can be manually operated. As in the slide production, it is possible to have an audible tone to signal the operator when it's time to change the frame. The change can be from a remote control, push-button switch, or manual operation at the machine. The automatic advance, with an inaudible signal, is so rapid that the viewer rarely sees the motion between frames.

There is a disadvantage, though, in the production of filmstrips. Since there must be a continuous film, the negative should be shot as a continuous entity, too. When shooting 75 to 100 shots, it's easy to forget one, to miss an overlay, or get one out of sequence. When this happens, the negative will be incorrect, and it is costly to produce a filmstrip from the two or three negatives required to correct the problem. Another disadvantage is that once the program is put together, it's not wise to splice in new shots. Not many projectors will take the spliced film. It's usually advisable to reshoot a new negative for each change, meaning an additional expense. The old film is no longer of value, since it really isn't profitable to try to use it in any way.

Overhead Projectors: Transparencies

Overhead projectors, so-called because the lens is on a stand over the item to be projected, offer a versatility which combines some of the features of the chalkboard with some of the advantages of the slide projector. One big advantage is that the room light can be left on (although light must not shine directly on the screen). This is a decided help to instructors, since they do not have to bother turning lights off and on. Also, going suddenly from a dark room to a bright one is slightly irritating to the students, and the overhead projector eliminates this problem.

When transparencies are shown on the overhead projector, trainers can write on the picture, cover up certain parts of it, and/or point with a pencil to whatever parts they wish, without going to the screen. The projector is designed with a wide angle lens so it can be used close to the front of the room, near the instructor. Some instructors prefer to sit beside the machine and teach from this position. This is generally the best arrangement, since it allows the students to see and enables the instructor to change his or her own transparencies. (Pictures in the overhead projector cannot be changed by remote control.)

With the proper equipment, overhead transparencies can be made in a matter of seconds, even from printed sheets or classroom notes. Some equipment even includes color in this quick process. Longer processes allow for more liberal use of color. Even photographs can be made into transparencies with the right developing processes.

The overhead projector has some disadvantages, as has been mentioned. One decided disadvantage is that it allows itself to be *misused easily*. When correctly used, it is very effective, but when misused, it is the least effective of all visual aids. For example, it is easy to simply reproduce whole letter-sized sheets in black and white; it can be done in a few seconds. But the result is often a very unsatisfactory, unexciting, and ineffective visual. Some instructors try to enhance such transparencies by covering up all but the line being discussed, and moving down the page a line at a time. This can be effective, sometimes, but it can also be tedious to the instructor and monotonous to the student, especially if the material is barely readable to begin with!

Another drawback is the necessity of having to be close to the equipment much of the time to change transparencies. Instructors lose their ability to move about and keep up interest with their movement. Also, *sitting and teaching* is an easy way to kill the enthusiasm of both the student and instructor. An experienced instructor can carry on a successful teaching session, but a supervisor coming from the job should not try to teach from a sitting position for very long. One caution: No member of the group should *ever* be asked to give up his or her opportunity to learn in order to change the transparencies for the instructor.

Video

The use of video has grown and improved rapidly in the last few years. It provides an immediate viewing of something that has just been filmed. Unlike the movie, there is no waiting time for developing, processing, and reproducing. Just as in the audio tape, video tape can be rewound and played back almost instantly. Like the movie, video is ideal for showing motion, or for showing things that need to be studied from a visual, rather than an audible standpoint. It takes only a little practice to get fairly proficient at using the equipment, and most of the tapes are now in cartridges of some kind, so storage is easy, though not inexpensive. The quality of the end product is good in both color and black and white Since most of us live in a "TV" world, students find little difficulty in looking at programs in that format. It's now possible to project to full-sized screens, if we have the equipment, so there isn't the problem of multiple monitors.

As good as it is, there is still misuse of video as a medium. Often it is used where sound would be all that is needed to do the teaching. In an interview, for instance, where we're trying to teach a sequence of questions, and are not concerned about body language, video has a serious drawback. Since sight is usually more attention getting than sound, the replay of the interview on video may cause the students to get more involved in looking than in listening.

Cost is still a factor to be reckoned with, though it is much lower, and the quality much better, than a few years ago. Compatability from one machine to the next is no longer much of a problem, and the limitations on the use of the equipment after it has been purchased is no longer cost but imagination.

Chalkboard

Nothing is more commonly used in the training room than the chalkboard, yet it is probably misused as often as it is used correctly. Why? Because, like the overhead projector, it lends itself to misuse. *The teacher has to develop good chalkboard habits and then consciously use them.*

The chalkboard is an excellent teaching aid, the teacher's real standby in any crisis. A diagram, a crude picture, a rough sketch can often help students who are uncertain of an idea to understand it quickly. The instructor can trace out the solution of a problem for a befuddled trainee in moments, then erase it and be ready for the next item of discussion. The instructor can place complex diagrams on the board, piece-by-piece, as the student easily follows each step. Where further explanation is needed, the instructor can add to an explanation or make changes with very little effort. Colored chalk can be used to show various components.

But all of this versatility is not without handicaps. The chalkboard is an open invitation for the trainers to violate almost all good training techniques. First, they can talk to the board instead of the group, thus losing eye contact and possibly cutting down their volume to the point where the people in the back row can't hear. In talking to the board, they may cover up what is written, so the students can't see it. Then their writing may be so small—or so poor—that no one can read it. What really frustrates trainees who are hurrying to copy down long lists or other information from the board is to have instructors erase the material when they are half-way through and casually say, "You won't need to write this down; I have copies for you."

The Easel

The paper easel or flip chart differs from the chalkboard in that information can be put on ahead of time and covered up, then it can be saved by merely turning the page. All the things said about the misuse of the chalkboard apply as well to the easel. Charts can be enlarged to easel size and placed in with the paper for handy reference. Caution should be taken, however, to see that the original chart (or copy to be enlarged) is readable. If the original isn't legible, the enlarged one may not be much better. By touching up the original the result can be improved, and touching up the enlargement will help even more. Color can be added to the enlarged copy to help bring out important points. The color should be meaningful, though, and should never be used just to have color. Misuse of color can emphasize an unimportant point, letting a significant fact or idea be lost because it is not in color. As with all visuals, the material on the easel should be *large enough to be seen, and simple enough to be understood.*

Demonstrations and Models

The easiest way to present information about a piece of gear is to have the actual item or a demonstration model in the classroom. This way the students can see the operation in "real life" rather than from pictures or drawings. They can even experiment with it, try to operate it, or perhaps repair it or adjust it in some way. Too often, however, the trainees are exposed to a demonstration which consists of knobs being twisted, levers pulled, lights turned on, etc., all of which is done by the instructor with perhaps only a handful of students able to see what is happening. The knobs are small, the levers secluded, and the lights labeled with small letters. Beyond the front row, no one can see anything well enough to really learn it. It is equally useless for the instructor to demonstrate the device while standing in front of it. By obstructing the view of the group the instructor makes it difficult for any of them to learn. It is not enough just to have a demonstration device in the classroom; *it must be seen and understood if it is to help the trainees learn.*

STUDENTS SHOULD HANDLE EQUIPMENT

Often the very device the employee uses on the job is brought into the training room—and the trainee is never allowed to actually work with it! If the terminal behavior set up in the objectives calls for proficiency in the operation of a piece of gear, or even the explanation of various parts, there is no substitute for having the trainees use the device itself. It may be that limitations of time or money make it impossible for *all* of them to work on the gear individually, but at least small groups of three or four working together are better than a whole class watching one person. The instructor can go through the operation once or twice, perhaps call on a volunteer to repeat all or portions of the operation, then break the class into small groups for further activity. The groups can be assigned time after class, lunch hours can be rotated, or even classtime may be allotted. While part of the class is working with the equipment, other parts of the class can be dealing with matters relating to the device, such as mathematical calculations, memorization of parts, or the listing of uses. The time should not be wasted. As will be noted in another chapter, these small group excercises can be very valuable learning experiences, and should be built into every course as time allows.

LABORATORY EXERCISES

Sometimes it's necessary to set up a laboratory to demonstrate certain elements of the job. Most of what has been said about demonstration devices applies equally to laboratory work. It must be seen to be appreciated; it must be a meaningful experience to the extent the trainee is expected to use it back on the job, and wherever possible the trainee should handle the equipment. Here again small-group exercises may be called for, so each person can feel a closer association with the experiments and demonstrations. While the students may enjoy just "fiddling" with the equipment, the exercise should be well planned and directed to accomplish a specific end. A laboratory instructor should be on hand to help in case there is a problem either with the equipment or learning. Incidentally, the style of instruction appropriate to the laboratory is different from that which goes best in the classroom, and often an individual who is ill at ease in the classroom becomes an excellent instructor when getting his hands on the gear used on the job.

KNOW THE EQUIPMENT

Regardless of whether the instructors are using a model, a demonstration device, or are in the laboratory, *they must know how the equipment works.* This means studying diagrams or schematics, if necessary, to understand the intricacies and peculiarities of each device used. If there are parts that may not always work, the instructor should either replace them or know what to do in case of failure. *Instructors should never try to teach with equipment they have not personally tested.* They should have at least one complete "dry run" before class time. The more practice they can get, the smoother the real show will go. One thing is certain: the trainees didn't come to the lab to watch the instructor fumble with equipment that works only sometimes. Of course, this holds true for anything used for instruction purposes, whether it be laboratory devices or projectors, or even a chalk-holder. What the instructors do well will probably contribute to learning; what they do poorly will surely detract from it. Instructors are in the classroom to promote learning, not prevent it.

INVOLVEMENT WITH VISUALS

Visuals are interesting and sometimes dramatic, but they are still rather static presentations. By themselves, they are no more than a glorified lecture, for the most part. They do not force involvement any more than a lecture does. They can easily be misused with the trainer thinking that he or she is doing a fine job with excellent visual aids. There is no doubt that many visuals are more exciting than a dull lecturer, but we need to apply the same principles to visual aids as we do to any form of teaching. There still needs to be feedback, and accountability, and involvement. Just because we're using visuals doesn't guarantee that learning will take place or that retention is automatic. Visuals don't allow for practice. Visuals don't force the students to try out a new skill. They do, however, tend to lull both the instructor and the learners into thinking that they have just witnessed a great learning experience.

What is needed is a way to build in involvement and accountability and feedback when showing a film or a filmstrip or a video tape, but it is very difficult to bring about these effects. At least we can stop a lecture and answer a question, or start a discussion, or go back over parts of the presentation where we saw puzzlement or disagreement. With the visuals, we don't even see the viewer until the presentation is over and the lights are turned on. Does this mean that learning doesn't take place with visuals—especially canned visuals? No, it just means that we have to work at promoting it. We have to build in the accountability. We can't just turn the projector on, say "Here's something you should find interesting," and show the film. Neither can we be successful when we say, "We've got about 15 minutes till break time. Let's look at this film, then break for awhile." Some instructors give tests after the film is over, building in accountability, involvement, and feedback in this way. The trouble with this is that the students don't know until the test is given that they should have looked and listened better, and we want learning to take place, not just get missed questions!

How about telling the students before the showing that they will be tested? That's a way of letting them know that they're going to be accountable, but we can't force learning by threatening with a test. A better way is to give them an assignment of some kind that can be done only by watching for things in the showing. Or they can be told, "When you're through, you'll need to fill out a form like the one described in the film we're about to show." That simple statement gives them a need for watching the film, and gets them involved in a meaningful way. Or, we can have them begin an assignment, get to a point where they can't progress further, then offer the film as a means of stretching their learning. Another way to get them involved is to stop the showing and deal with activities from the film. If it's a technical film, stop and ask for expansion or examples from past experience. If it's a case-study type of film, there may be suitable places for stopping for discussion, or perhaps we should consider replaying after the discussion, stopping at particular events where we think learning can be furthered.

If none of these methods is appropriate, it sometimes is helpful to ask the group to look for specific things in the showing. We ask them to "find the objections, or three main points, or ways of overcoming the problems, or the pros and cons of doing it this way." We can break the group into two subgroups and give competitive assignments: one to agree, the other to disagree with the findings in the film. If we have difficulty making the students accountable, we might want to consider just what it is we're hoping to accomplish by showing the film. There is always the possibility that the audio-visual doesn't add anything to the learning process, and that we can't really find a good reason for showing it or using it!

Exercises and Questions

1. Questions for discussion: Do most instructors *really* believe visual aids increase learning? Why aren't more visuals used? Does it take *more* or *less* time to teach a subject using visuals?

2. There is evidence to show that the learning produced is not proportional to the sophistication of the visual. In other words, more color, more detail in the artwork, a greater number of actual photographs don't necessarily increase learning on a direct "straight-line" improvement basis. This means that the instructor could use *more* visuals than usual, since they don't have to be so elaborate. Have subgroups of three or four people prepare—using easel paper—some visual aids to teach a simple subject selected by them. Someone in each

subgroup should teach the subject using the aid. When the sessions are over, each subgroup should be prepared to defend the approach it took, and why a visual was needed.

3. With the use of "brainstorming" techniques, come up with effective ways of teaching visual aids to a group of prospective instructors. Remember: this isn't an attempt to teach them *how* to use visuals. The objective is "they will use visual aids in the classroom that increase learning. They will do it because they are convinced that visual aids are necessary (in most cases) to produce adequate learning."

4. By group activity, come up with a list of as many kinds of visual aids as possible. Discuss the advantages and disadvantages of each. Rank each in order of ease of *use*. Now rank each in order of *effectiveness*. Finally, rank according to *cost*. Using these three rankings as guides, pick up the top three choices as the most valuable visuals to use.

chapter 12
TESTING

All too often, testing in the industrial classroom is looked on with disdain. It is unfortunate that this attitude exists, however, because testing is *very close to the end result of our training efforts.* If on-the-job performance is considered testing, then this *is* the end result. The problem is that both instructors and students fail to give testing its proper place in the classroom. They often do not understand either how to test or why to test. In this chapter we will deal less with theories of testing than with the use of tests as an integral part of the training activity.

WHY TEST?

Some have taken the easy way out and said, "After all, these employees are adults and responsible individuals. They resent being treated like children with tests and exams." (A wise philosopher has said only *children* resent being treated like children!) If testing is considered merely as a means of obtaining a grade (which will later be used by a supervisor in lieu of management judgment) or as a necessary evil at the end of a course, it certainly should be resented—and not because it's "childish treatment," either. Testing has its place in training as a means of evaluating well-defined objectives. In fact, properly prepared objectives will most likely include testing procedures and specify satisfactory test results.

There are many reasons for testing, but the primary reason is that *testing is a means of getting feedback on learning.* It gives us feedback not only on the trainee's performance, but on that of the instructor as well. Tests show us who has learned (and to some degree how much was learned); they show us which teaching methods produced the most learning with the most students, and which techniques didn't work so well. Without these measurements, our future training is left up to chance. We can only guess what is good and what isn't. No conscientous instructor would want to face a group of trainees knowing no more about his or her techniques than this. Testing has an interesting side effect which is beneficial to all concerned; almost regardless of how and when it is used, it *motivates* the students. It matters not whether the grades are taken, whether the scores are sent back to the supervisors, or even if the rest of the group sees the grades; the ego of the trainee almost always causes him or her to want to do well on the test. The alert instructor should learn to take advantage of this fact.

So testing can be used to motivate. But it is dangerous to think of tests as motivators, because it is easy to lose sight of their real purpose—to provide *feedback on learning*. When tests are used only as motivators they take on an almost sinister attribute. The instructor begins to think of them as being punitive, or he or she uses them as threats. In this light it is no wonder that testing is feared by adults and children alike. But tests, used in their proper place and for the proper purpose, do motivate. Trainees, knowing in advance they are to be tested, will study harder, listen more closely, and generally learn more. Discounting the usual amount of frustration that develops over tests, we are left with the fact that students will adapt to and accept *good* testing.

WHO IS TESTED?

To say to the student "It's really the instructor who's being tested," is closely akin to telling a child "This hurts me worse than it does you," as he or she is subjected to a razor strap. The student knows very well who is being tested, and has no illusions that he or she is merely furnishing data on the instructor's performance. Even if this were so, it isn't likely the trainee could ever be convinced of it. Nevertheless, the instructor *does* get tested with the tests taken by his or her students. It's very easy for a teacher to look at a pile of low-score papers and remark, "This sure was a poor group." Not many people would even dispute such a remark, for the truth is, it may actually have been a poor group.

But the group may have had a poor instructor!

If the instructor knew the students—their backgrounds, job experience and learning capabilities,—knew what he or she wanted them to be able to do back on the job, and if *the entire group* made a poor showing on a valid test, he or she would know almost certainly that the fault was in the teaching process, not in the students. If all the class did well except for one or two members, then there is evidence that the couple who did poorly may be at fault. But even then they might not be at fault if (1) the other members of the group already knew the information when they started the course, (2) the one or two low-scorers had inadequate background, insufficient experience, etc., or (3) the teacher failed to recognize that they needed help early in the course and failed to help them.

When a test is given at the end of some presentation period, many things are tested besides the instructor and the trainees. The time allotted to subject matter comes under scrutiny; was their enough time to meet the specified objectives? Was the instructor fighting a losing battle by having to pass up questions in order to cover the material, all the time knowing that the questions indicated a lack of understanding of what had been said already?

Or perhaps there was enough time, but poor scheduling and improper planning had allowed more time than was needed for some subjects and not enough for others.

So *timing* gets tested right along with the students.

So *does the classroom itself.* The ventilation, visibility, and acoustics all play a part in the learning process. How good were these things during the training sessions? If the air became so stuffy that the group became drowsy or uncomfortable, then the tests may indicate poor learning for this period. If the classroom was so designed that some of the students could not *see* the board or screen very well, this is likely to be reflected in their test scores. The same is true if they could not *hear.* Furthermore, if the chairs were uncomfortable, or if there was an undue amount of distraction in and about the classroom during the teaching sessions, the trainees will surely do worse on the test than they would have under ideal circumstances.

ARE TESTS NECESSARY?

Many things, then, are reflected in the test results. Unfortunately, it isn't always easy to tell just what caused low scores on a test; it's even possible that *the test itself may be at fault.* The question could be raised, "Is testing really useful, since there are so many variables?" The answer is, "Yes, when you cut down on the variables!" There is no reason to tolerate extraneous noises, poor lighting, bad acoustics, improper visibility, and uncomfortable classroom conditions. These things can be determined with no real effort, and if there is any doubt, the trainees can give a quick and accurate evaluation of these items. These variables can and should be eliminated, after which they will have no effect on testing.

Tests are useful and necessary because some kind of feedback is required to measure learning effectiveness. Ideally, they would be unnecessary if the individual were measured back on the job by his or her supervisor. Unfortunately, however, supervisors are not adequately trained to give valid feedback to the instructor. They can tell if the employee is performing better, but not *how much better,* at least not immediately. This is even more true if the learning was supposed to include a large amount of factual information. (Obviously, if the result was to be *higher* production, *more* sales, etc., the supervisor has a yardstick by which to measure, and so is the only one who can give the correct feedback.)

USE SHORT QUIZZES OCCASIONALLY

What about matters of scheduling and timing? How can we know if these things influenced the testing? One easy way is to build in some "spot" testing along the way, especially at significant points. Short, specific quizzes, designed to give feedback on the subjects under consideration (and not broad generalities), and included as part of the regular class work, will furnish invaluable information. Because they are short, the quizzes are less painful; because they are fitted into the regular schedule, they do not cause anxiety. But the instructor will obtain much needed information from them at a time when he or she can do something about it, and with a minimum of variables acting on the results.

The idea of testing in small samples has another advantage; it gets the trainees involved and has them participating at more frequent intervals. The procedure is amazingly simple for the excellent results obtained. The instructor, who has scheduled the test in his or her notes and has the questions (two or three) written out, simply says, "Get a piece of paper and see what you can do with these questions." The instructor may hand them out, or read them, or write them on the board if time permits, or show them on an overhead projector. whatever method is used, the whole thing needs to be casual rather than very formal. It should be (and should appear to be) a regular part of the class activity. After a few experiences like this, the class will be adjusted to them and will take them without great concern. The students will, of course, still want to do well, so the feedback will be an accurate measure of their learning.

By giving these short quizzes periodically, instructors will know where any weak spots in their teaching approach may be. If they give enough tests, they can discover their shortcomings in time to give remedial work or repeat certain portions of the course with a different approach. Instructors need not feel it necessary to test every item if their periodic short tests reveal that the students are learning well.

WHY DO STUDENTS DREAD TESTS?

Perhaps nothing in education is more universally frustrating to students than the circumstances surrounding testing. Success or failure, going on or staying behind, even being accepted or rejected have always been associated with tests. There is no mystery why students, even adults, fear tests. In reality, it is not the tests they fear but the use of the results. Every child who has had to "give up playing every afternoon for a month because of that grade in geography" knows why he or she doesn't like to take tests.

The teacher must learn to overcome this dread by showing that the results are for evaluating all aspects of the training. It should not be a surprise to trainees that they are expected to learn material presented to them, especially when the company is footing the bill for the time away from the job. Even if the scores become a part of the permanent record and influence the trainee's future progress with the company, *it is possible to overcome certain fears about testing.*

THE STUDENT WANTS FAIRNESS

One major reason why trainees dread tests is that tests are often administered *unfairly.* Not intentionally, of course, but because so many elements surrounding testing lend themselves to unfair testing. To begin with, it is difficult to find a standard for the accurate measurement of knowledge gained. To give ten questions and let each count ten points just to make one hundred points is usually an unfair approach. This says that each question is exactly weighted to one-tenth of the whole; that each question has the same merit, the same value as every other question. It says, too, that these ten questions are the most representative available (or equal to any other). To grade in this manner is to say that a student making 90 on the test has learned 90% of *all* information presented over the period covered by the test. No teacher is willing to be held to these strict rules, *and yet that is the way we most often grade.*

Next, unfairness is quite possible in the teaching itself. Students realize when they are being short-changed in instruction. They can tell good teaching from bad teaching. When they have been exposed to bad training, then are held accountable for it (while the teacher gets off free), they feel they are being treated unfairly. And they feel this with good reason.

Another problem in fairness lies in deciding how long students should be given to show how much they have learned. If testing is for feedback, do we want to know how much the students have learned *totally,* or are we interested only in how much of what they have learned they can feed back to us in an hour?

We are quick to admit that some people *learn* more slowly than others, but do we take into consideration the possibility that some may *feed back* their learning more slowly than others? A trainee who knows an answer but does not have time to adequately express himself or herself on a test is going to resent it for a long time.

The teacher who is aware of these things can correctly interpret test results. When most of the class miss a question, it can probably be pinned on the instruction. When only one or two miss something, they are most likely at fault. Evidence from previous short quizzes will give additional information. One interesting thing is the fact that many instructors worry if *all* of their students get the questions right. They seem to prefer some kind of "curve" with lows and highs. *The good instructor should teach so well that all trainees make excellent scores.* Such an instructor should be especially pleased when this happens.

TESTS NEED NOT BE FEARED

When the trainees find out that the instructor is trying to be fair, and to get accurate measurements of what has been learned, they will be more comfortable about tests. When they take enough short tests along the way, they become more at ease with tests. If the instructor will remove as many threats as possible from the test results, the fears will subside further. If the tests are well worded, not ambiguous, and if they really cover the material accurately, the students will feel they are being treated fairly. Finally, if the tests are not tedious and lengthy, and if enough time is allowed to adequately answer the questions, most trainees will accept testing for what it is—a necessary part of the teaching-learning process.

TESTING BY SAMPLING

There are two ways of finding out what has been learned, by a superficial test on all items or by sampling in depth on some items. (It is possible, of course, to use a combination of the two.) All tests use one or both of these methods. Since it usually isn't possible to test all items in depth, instructors who want to know whether the student really can do the things set up in the objectives may resort to a sampling process. That is, they assume that if they test on a random basis, they will have a fairly accurate picture of the *total* learning that took place. They then make no effort to test *all* items; but rely on their sampling to give them accurate results, which it should.

There are at least two disadvantages to sampling, both of which can be overcome. First, instructors must resist teaching the material covered by the random questions to the exclusion of the other items. In fact, it is better if they don't even know which questions will be used on the test, because then they will be free to cover *all* the subjects. Second, the student should not be left with the impression that certain parts of the course are more important than others because they appeared on the quiz. Teachers must take care to show that *all* parts are important, not just those appearing on the test. They should also explain the testing process without apologies. After all, it is the method being used, and the trainees have a right to know it.

WHAT IS A GOOD TEST?

The characteristics of a good test make a long list. Good tests have questions that cannot be misunderstood, are easy to read and understand, and require straightforward answers. Good tests cover the subject without being too long. Good tests are easy to score, and the results are meaningful. They leave no room for doubts about the correct answer, and when shown the right answer the trainee can immediately see its correctness. The terms or words in the test are never indefinite and statements never contain double negatives or tricky words with hidden meanings.

The list could go on, but none of this is new to anyone who has ever been a student. Is it possible for instructors to ever have their tests meet all these criteria? Probably not, but a little conscientious effort will go a long way toward making better tests. Teachers must ask themselves, "Do these questions really test the objectives of the course?" As has been said, the ideal situation would be for instructors to *teach* on the objectives and for someone else to *test* on them.

Since it is rarely possible to have these conditions, teachers can do one of two things. *Before* the course is prepared, they can make up a series of questions they feel will test for the objectives. Then they should forget these questions and design the course to teach the objectives. If the students do not pass the test, then the course should be changed. A second approach, if the course has already been prepared, is to look realistically at the objectives and prepare a test that will accurately measure the behavior of the students against the objectives. Again it is the *course* that should be taught, not the test questions.

A "good" test, then, is simply *one that accurately measures how well the students have met the objectives.*

But what about the short quizzes? Do they test objectives also? No instructor should go into a classroom, even for an hour's session, without asking himself or herself "What do I want the class to be able to do when I finish this session?" The objectives may not be written down (although they should certainly include the material for each specific topic or category of instruction), but teachers should have a clear mental picture of exactly what their purpose is for each training effort. If they know what they want the students to be able to do at the end of a given time, any short quiz they may plan to give should cover the objectives. The instructors want the student to *demonstrate* his or her learning in some way, in some manner. If instructors cannot specify what learning should take place, they cannot measure it. If they can tell what is to be learned, they should be able to test for it.

THINGS NOT TESTED BY TESTS

Given at the end of the course, the best test ever prepared will not measure how much the trainees knew when they *first came into the class.* Tests do not necessarily measure learning that has taken place in a specific classroom, unless the class was tested *before* the instructor started. Teachers have been fooled by students who scored excellent results on a final quiz, when the truth was that they already knew the material and were bored most of the time. Also, students with low scores have been considered poor students, when in reality they may have come a long way, but were very far behind to start with. Often instructors will prepare "pre-tests," similar in value to the final test (or the sum of individual tests during the course), so as to get an accurate evaluation of the trainees' progress.

Another thing not shown by tests is how much the students *could have learned with a better* instructor. Teachers are almost always prone to evaluate students in absolute terms. They will say, "This class did very well for its capabilities." Rarely do they say, "I did very well for *my* capabilities." The students are measured as though every item, every subject, every skill was presented in such a way that they *should have gotten it.* While it is not true that "when a student fails a teacher has failed," it is true that teachers could do better, and some are better than others. This means that the same group, under the same conditions, *could do better* under one instructor than under another. Unfortunately, it isn't possible to test instructors that easily. The fact remains, though, that tests indicate, but do not accurately measure, how well the students could have done with the best possible instruction. Maybe they had the best possible instruction—but the tests will not reveal it!

WHAT TO DO WITH TEST RESULTS

What good are test scores? Who should see them? Unless pretests have been used, the test shows only where the students are now, at the end of the training period. Often this is exactly what we want to know—what they can do now. If this is all, then we simply say they are qualified to do the job prescribed back home, or they aren't. The test results substantiate the conclusion.

But strange things sometimes happen with grades.

Not everyone is qualified to use test scores wisely, not because they lack intelligence, but because they may not know what was in the course, in the test, or required by the instructor. Invariably, one use becomes a comparison of one trainee with another or several who have attended the same course. A 93'er is better than a 91'er, although the median grade may have been

67. A 90 sounds better than an 89, but 89 sounds about the same as an 88.

Company policy usually dictates the use of grades, but the teacher should be careful to find out who uses the grades and for what purpose. A supervisor who observes two people on a job for a year is in a better position to judge two employees than is a teacher who sees them for only a few days. Test results may not reveal that one had a headache on the day of the test, or that one had a sick baby back home, and couldn't concentrate during the course. *Test scores for classroom training are rarely comprehensive enough to serve as a substitute for management decisions in judging employees.*

WHAT KIND OF TESTS SHOULD BE USED?

There are many good reference books available on different kinds of tests and their relative merits. No effort will be made here to discuss the advantages and disadvantages of the various testing methods. However, a few cautions should be noted.

First, if the scores of the tests are going to be used as information on permanent personnel records, the instructor should know it, and should make every effort to have valid scores on performance. If the scores are only to be used for quick measurement during the training session, the teacher need not be so painstaking.

The kind of test to use is the kind that best tests the subject matter, balanced against the time available for testing and grading. For instance, an essay-type test might be the best means of seeing whether the students have all the fine points of a subject, but if the time allowed for the test is not enough to let the trainees write down all that they should, how can the test be valid? On the other hand, a true-false test may be quick to take and quick to grade, but it may not really test whether the students can make necessary discriminations. The teacher is forced, then, to compromise between both, perhaps using some true-false, some essay.

The instructor should avoid some of the obvious pitfalls of all types of tests. For instance, the "false" side of a true-false test does not always test whether the trainee knows the "true" side. To say, "So-and-so is the *first* thing to do," with the answer "false" only shows that the trainee knows that "so-and-so" is *not* first. It does not test to see if he or she knows what does come first.

Multiple-choice questions are hard to prepare, because all answers should sound plausible. The trainer may run out of good choices and resort to, "all of the above," or "none of the above." This is generally an admission that not enough choices could be found. This does not rule out multiple-choice, however, because in many cases such questions allow for the testing of necessary discriminations. Care should be taken to prepare them well and to provide good, logical choices.

Whatever kind of testing is used, the same rules should apply: Be sure the test measures the students' performance ability. Be sure the results are in terms of what they know is right, not just what they know isn't right. Be sure they can adequately express themselves within the framework of the tests. After all, the teacher wants to know what the students know—the tests should support this aim, not block it.

TEACHING WITH TESTS?

Instructors are often heard to remark, "Tests are another tool in the teaching chest," meaning that the instructor can teach with testing. The statement is valid to some extent, but the teacher should be cautious about blandly saying that is the purpose of testing. It is only a by-product, not the main function. To come to the end of a teaching session in which learners were supposed to have learned all about a subject, then give a test and say it is "for teaching" leaves the instructor in a bad light.

Suppose, on the other hand, that short quizzes are given, then reviewed in class. In such a case the *test material* is used for learning, but the test itself really is for the evaluating of learning. Calling a test "a teaching tool" often is a means of covering up *bad tests and poor teaching.* Perhaps the only condition under which testing can be called teaching is when *every* item is tested and the trainees know they are getting the right answer. This becomes self-instruction and in reality is "programed learning."

The point is that the instructor should be satisfied to let tests do what they do best—measure learning. There are plenty of other tools that the supervisor-become-teacher has to master. Getting tests to measure accurately will be an accomplishment in itself; the teacher should be happy to have achieved this much success without asking the tests to do even more!

Exercises and Questions

1. List as many *reasons* as possible for testing. List as many *ways* as possible of testing. Looking at these two lists, check the reasons and ways most often used in your situation. Why are some used more than others?

2. Questions for discussion: Instructors often are heard to say, "I think testing is an excellent teaching tool," even though the test comes at the end of the teaching situation. Is it possible that testing is *not* a teaching tool in this case?

3. Students sometimes complain that "It isn't fair to give me a grade based on 100 since the instructing was less than that, and so was the quality of the test." Discuss the validity of this complaint.

4. In subgroups, prepare a test for someone studying a unit on testing. On a rotation basis, give the test to one of the other subgroups. After each has finished taking the test, discuss what *behavior* was being tested. Could you tell from the tests what the objective might have been for *teaching* such a unit?

5. Using Question 4 as a guide, list the requirements for good testing, including length, types, and method of administration.

chapter 13
EFFECTIVE SPEAKING

A good speaker and a good instructor are not necessarily the same thing. Some people, in preparing supervisors to be teachers, spend too much time on speech training. There are two dangers here: first, if too much time is spent on speech training, some other subject, just as vital, may be sacrificed; second, the prospective teachers may be misled into thinking that lecturing is their main purpose in the classroom. *It is probably accurate, however, to say that a bad speaker is a bad teacher.*

WORDS MUST BE HEARD

It would be an odd situation indeed if the teacher did not have to use words to communicate with the students (unless the entire course was built around programed instruction). Words are the means of communication. As was said earlier, they are the *codes* we use to transmit ideas, thoughts, concepts, etc. But they must be heard to be understood; they must be heard clearly to be clearly understood; they must be heard in their entirety if the student is to have total understanding.

Different people have different *natural* speech patterns. Some have naturally loud voices, while others normally speak in voices that do not carry well in the classroom. While volume alone does not guarantee clarity, voices with little volume cannot be heard, even if the words are quite clear. Rarely does an instructor talk too loud, but often trainers fail to talk above the sound of a projector or outside interference. What may sound loud to the instructor may be too soft for the back row.

Teachers who discover that their voice is too soft for the entire class to hear must make special effort to raise their voice level all the time. But they may tire after speaking for a while, and find it difficult to keep their voice volume up. The voice, like water, seeks its own level. If the teacher has a naturally soft voice, it will always tend to revert to softness, and conscious effort must be made to keep it loud enough.

How can the instructor know she's being heard? The answer is actually very simple. If she knows she has a tendency to speak too softly, she asks one of the people on the back row to let her know if her voice drops below an audible level. The students will appreciate this conscientiousness on the part of the teacher. If she still has doubts, the instructor can write herself messages in the margin of her notes as reminders to "speak louder," "check on back row hearing," "speak up!", etc.

SPEAK CLEARLY

Clarity of speech is not an accidental thing. All of us tend to become lazy with our pronunciation and enunciation. This laziness causes us to slur words, run words together, and generally speak in such a way that we can't be understood. Again, speaking so words can be understood is the result of *conscious* effort. It is possible to train our voices, however, to be both louder and clearer. Even so, we can still become lax and ease this habit. There is a simple way to check ourselves for clarity—practice a portion of a presentation with a tape recorder. Nothing gives a truer picture than a recording of the real thing. Play it back while you sit in the back of the room. Do the words come through clearly enough? Are there any distracting words or phrases that keep cropping up? Do you have any speech mannerisms that may trouble the students? When the recording is being made, be sure to speak *as to a class*, not just into the recorder. The results should reveal your natural voice, rather than one affected by a microphone and recorder.

ENTHUSIASM IS CATCHING

Nothing generates enthusiasm like enthusiasm. Supervisors who come to the classroom to teach aren't likely to be great dynamos in speaking, but they should radiate more than an average interest in their subject. They don't need to have the drive to produce a three-ring circus, but neither should they just collapse on the speaker's stand and deliver an hour's lecture in a monotone.

There are several ways in which instructors can show the trainees that they are interested in them and the subject.

First, there is *movement*. The students deserve to know an instructor is still awake by seeing him move occasionally. When the instructor leaves the speaker's stand, goes to the board or easel, crosses in front of the class, or even makes an occasional casual trip down the aisle, he puts more life in the presentation and enlivens the students. This doesn't mean the teacher is to be a homeless nomad; it means that he knows the subject well enough so that he does not have to stay glued to his notes. It means, too, that he wants to share his knowledge with the group, and if movement will help, he'll move.

Another indicator of enthusiasm is *voice inflection*. We cannot over-emphasize the importance of varying pitch and pace of the voice. Again, the speaker isn't supposed to develop into a silver-tongued orator. But it will be difficult for the speaker to impress a group with enthusiasm when his or her voice never varies from a continuous monotone. As we said earlier, speech needs punctuation just as badly as writing does. Pauses allowing time for thought, loudness on key words, repetition to call attention to important facts—all of these are forms of emphasis *and show enthusiasm.*

A subtle indicator of enthusiasm is the establishment of rapport with the trainees. The instructor who is enthusiastic about the subject wants the trainees to be likewise. He or she realizes that to bring about this enthusiasm he must establish a good relationship with the trainees. Such a relationship need not be based on friendship, necessarily, but on the feeling that the instructor knows the problems of the trainees and can provide the solutions to those problems. To bring about this rapport the instructor must never "talk down" to the trainees. He must make them feel that they are a real part of his class, and he is really there to help them.

Enthusiasm can be a quiet thing. It can be demonstrated by easy efficiency which is born of a teacher's confidence in himself. The teacher who knows his subject and who believes when he finishes teaching, that the students should know it also will develop self-enthusiasm and enthusiasm in the students.

A final word about enthusiasm. *Objectives* play an important role in the instructor's entire attitude toward his training activity. He should ask himself each time, just before starting a session, "What is it they should be able to do when I am finished an hour from now?" This personal challenge should pick up his own enthusiasm and send him into class with the right attitude.

He has by now determined what kind of behavior he expects to produce in the students, and he knows the time allotted to accomplish this objective. Therefore he will eliminate insignificant items from his instruction and stick to the subject. Also, and most important, he will look constantly for *feedback from the students.* He wants to know what they can do, what they know, what they understand. He worries when they don't understand something and looks for new and better ways of explaining a point. In short he has now become concerned with the learning in his classroom. Enthusiasm is the natural consequence of such concern.

WHAT ABOUT HUMOR?

The question of humor really shouldn't come up in a training situation. Not because it shouldn't be used, but because, to be effective, *it should be natural.* This means if humor naturally fits a situation, it should be used. If not, it should be left out. A person who cannot tell jokes will usually lose more than she will gain by trying to tell them. On the other hand, an excellent story-teller may get carried away with her success with humor and lose sight of her objectives and time limitations.

Crude humor and filthy stories have no place in a training situation, but subtle jokes and anecdotes that fit the occasion are most helpful. Humor provides a good change of pace, and a well-placed humorous remark can relax the trainees and open the way for further instruction. There is nothing wrong with letting the students know that the instructor is human, and humor is a good way to show this. *Humor should never ridicule the trainees,* especially any one of them in particular, unless it is clearly understood that the instructor is only kidding, and no reprimand is intended. On the other hand, it is always safe for trainers to ridicule themselves; it often helps to establish the rapport mentioned earlier.

LECTURING VERSUS TEACHING

As has already been said, the instructor is not expected to be a polished orator. However, he is expected to develop his speaking talents beyond the straight read-from-notes lecturing. Since effective speaking isn't necessarily effective teaching, the instructor must look for the things that best do his job. On a stage before hundreds of listeners, a forceful lecturer can sway his audience and have great influence on its behavior. But there is some doubt about how much of the response is emotional, and how much is the result of what is recalled from the lecture. In any case, the classroom is seldom an appropriate place for this kind of oratory.

Does this mean that the teacher can never lecture? Of course not. It means that "lecture" needs to be redefined and the stigma taken from it, if possible. One would be hard put to make a distinction between lecturing at a rostrum and teaching at a chalkboard. Lecture has become synonymous with standing in one place for long periods of time and talking without aids of any kind. Yet "lecturers" frequently use easels, chalkboards, even projected visuals.

It's better to think of lecturing as an activity that *does not require student participation*. Taken in this light, it is easier to see where lectures fit and where they do not. There are times when the instructor must do the talking because he has a series of facts that must be presented properly. In a few minutes he can review and reconstruct the same facts with the aid of trainee feedback. For a while he must lecture. *But not for long*. There is a limit to how long the trainees can stay involved without participating, but if the instructor speaks clearly, pleasantly, with force enough to be heard, he can hold the group longer than a poor speaker could. If he uses such techniques as change of pace, emphasis, motion, etc., he will be able to keep interest high even without trainee participation.

BEWARE THE SPEAKER'S STAND

One ominous item in the classroom is the speaker's stand, or lectern. Though inanimate, *it represents the downfall of many a potentially good instructor.* One word characterizes the action (or lack of action) around the stand—*rest.* Papers, notes, scripts *rest* on the stand; the speaker *rests* his hands, arms, elbows on the stand. The stand then becomes a *resting place.* But the instructor isn't in the room to rest, any more than the students are in the room to sleep. The instructor is there to teach; the students are there to learn.

The speaker's stand can kill enthusiasm more effectively than any other single item in the classroom. When the instructors lose their enthusiasm, the student's interest usually follows close behind. The speaker's stand is too convenient for relaxing. Instructors, perhaps in an effort to appear relaxed, may almost collapse on the stand. They may drape themselves over it and go on for hours without any sign of life except a monotonous voice. Trainees finally cease trying to follow such instructors— they have to struggle just to keep awake. The instructors, unintentionally of course, actually kill their own presentation because they haven't learned to use the stand correctly.

Some instructors have a tendency to use the stand as a "security rail" between themselves and the trainees. Being somewhat unsure of themselves, and perhaps suffering a little from stage fright, this type of instructor finds some comfort in standing behind the stand and gripping it with both hands. Whether he or she feels a sense of domination over the trainees by being above them, or feels protected behind the stand, he or she is likely to use the stand as often as possible. The well-prepared instructor should be equally at ease *with or without* the stand.

Used correctly, the stand is a means of keeping the attention at the front of the room. Instructors visit it occasionally to refresh their memory on facts and figures and to make sure of their order of presentation, and perhaps their timing. Good instructors are no more dependent on the stand than they are on long lecture notes. They feel at ease in front of the group, at the easel, at the chalkboard, or behind the speaker's stand. They need no crutch or resting place. They are free to put their hands or arms on the stand because they don't depend on it for rest or support. They do it because *it is natural at that time.*

OTHER MISUSES OF THE SPEAKER'S STAND

Some instructors collapse on the stand, some seem to crouch behind it, but others seem determined to *overpower* it. They attack the stand with a vengeance, wrapping legs and arms around it almost in a death struggle. They may almost topple it forward by climbing up on it. They may walk all over the base of the stand. Some use it to prop up a toe or scrape a heel, constantly looking down to see what is happening. Some seem to be content to just rock the stand. They tilt it forward, then from side to side. If it is light enough, some may even carry the stand around with them, trying to relocate it or line it up with some imaginary guidelines. The point of mentioning these things is obvious; they may be casual habits to the instructor, but they are a great distraction to the students. What a shame that such little things may cause a student to miss an opportunity to learn!

DISTRACTIONS MAY BE HABITS

Misusing the speaker's stand may distract the students, but other habits may be just as bad. There are many of them, and most are obvious. Jingling change, twirling string, tossing chalk, fiddling with a pencil, waving the pointer like a baton—all fall into this category. Even though the action may be natural and the instructor relaxed, the trainees may not be able to ignore these distractions. Most of these actions develop from nervousness in the beginning, then become habitual. Instructors are so used to them they don't realize what they are doing. *They can rid themselves of these habits only by a conscious effort,* and unless they are careful, the habit will come back when the conscious effort is stopped.

COMBINING SPEAKING AND VISUAL AIDS

Visual aids are a natural part of the classroom and should be a natural part of the instructor's presentation. However useful they are as a teaching aid, they should always be thought of as *learning aids*. They are for the benefit of the student, not the teacher. When teachers start to fit their aids into their training program, they should design them to *supplement, complement,* and *reinforce* the verbal efforts. The visuals should fit naturally into the routine, not be forced in because the instructor's consciences tell them they should use some visual aids.

Instructors never had a better friend in the classroom than a good set of visuals. Properly used, visuals give them a change of pace that makes instruction interesting; properly designed, they can serve as notes and reminders of what comes next, and summaries of what has gone before.

Instructors should never let the visuals control them, but rather *aid* instruction. Visuals should not interfere with the smooth flow of information. In other words, the trainees really shouldn't notice any point of transition between instruction *without* visuals and instruction *with* them. As the visuals come into view, whether on a screen or easel, the instructor should be sure that the students' eyes are directed to the proper place, then with only enough words to explain what is being shown, the instructor continues the teaching process in a natural manner.

If projected pictures are to be used, it is always an excellent idea to be sure everything is ready and checked out ahead of time. Ideally, all controls for lights and equipment should be at the instructor's fingertips so the instructor can go immediately into the visuals without undue delay and fumbling. Since the operation of the equipment should not hinder the instructor, automatic equipment is always desirable, with remote control for the instructor's use.

When charts or other material have been "pre-boarded" on an easel, teachers should be sure to make the pages in such a way that they can find the desired sheet without long delays for searching. This may mean putting tabs on the edge of the pages with some kind of markings for a cue. As the teacher needs a chart or a certain page, a glance at the tabs will show the correct place. It should be remembered, though, that visuals are aids, not the entire instruction. When there is nothing left for the group to learn from the picture or chart, *cover it up* or turn the projector off. Trainees have learned that pictures are to be looked at, and as long as they see something on a screen or easel, they probably will continue to look at it.

CAN TEACHERS LEARN TO SPEAK EFFECTIVELY?

The necessity for speaking well has already been mentioned. It should be noted here that "effective-speaking" in the classroom is *speaking that allows the students to learn.* It does not have to reach to the depth of the soul nor sway the audience to accomplish great things; it does not even have to qualify for an award in a public-speaking contest. In the classroom the instructor's speech has only to convey the proper thought, idea, concept, or skill. The instructor's posture, mannerisms, and body movements fall in the same category; all should be directed at helping the students learn, not impressing them with the trainer's oratorical excellence.

Instructors should strive always to be conscious of their actions in the classroom—whether these include speech, movement, or the use of visual aids. If they have any doubts about their ability, they should get another instructor to sit in during a class session and give an honest critique. The use of the tape recorder for voice training has already been discussed.

There is a final effective way for instructors to measure their speaking ability. All things considered, *is the group learning as well as can be expected?* Are they staying alert? Are they responding at the proper places? Do they appear bored? Are the people on the back row straining to hear? Is the group alive or listless? The answers to these and similar questions will go a long way toward telling instructors how good their speaking technique is. In fact, they will probably tell how good an instructor really is!

Exercises and Questions

1. Some have claimed that a teacher must be a good public speaker in order to be effective. Others cite examples of poor speakers who were good teachers. Discuss the relationship between "public speaking" and "effective teaching."

2. Discuss the word "enthusiastic" in the following statement: "I like Joe as an instructor. He's really a live wire; moves

around, up and down the aisle, uses his arms and hands. I don't think you can beat an enthusiastic instructor!"

Is this the only way to show enthusiasm? Is it possible that students sometimes "like" an instructor because he keeps them awake rather than because they learn more?

3. The speaker's stand has often been called the "enemy of good teaching." List all the misuses of a speaker's stand. Why have it at all? Do some instructors use it as a "security blanket"?

4. What (if any) is the difference in the objectives of good teaching and public speech?

chapter 14
CLASSROOM TECHNIQUES

So far we have discussed many aspects of "effective teaching." In this chapter we will look at some simple techniques that will help prospective instructors feel more in touch with their assignment. A word of caution, though. There is no single answer for the question, "What techniques do I have to be a good instructor?" *There is no stereotype for a good instructor.* What works for one person may cause another to be a failure.

These points were covered in detail in Chapter 1. They are mentioned again to remind the supervisor (who is seeking help in becoming an effective instructor) that he or she must not rely on one method *just because it sounds good, or works for someone else!* Pick a technique and try it. It just may work for a certain instructor at a certain time. Another technique may even work better. There are some things that every instructor can use to improve classroom effectiveness. It is up to the individual to select and use those things that fit *his* or *her* personality, course content, and particular group of trainees.

GET THE CLASS ON YOUR SIDE

For some strange reason, there is often an odd form of competition in the classroom—not among individual students, but between the students and the instructor. Whatever the cause, the alert instructor will very quickly try to eliminate this feeling. It is not enough, either, to just say, "Remember, people, I'm on your side." The instructor must quickly *demonstrate* a willingness to help them learn.

Nothing impresses a class quicker than an instructor who causes them to learn. The instructor who can come into the classroom, quickly get the trainees involved, and just as quickly produce some learning has gone a long way toward winning over the class. Students want to learn, they like to learn, and the person who gets them to do it in a hurry becomes a sort of hero to them.

Instructors should not try to get the students on their side by ridiculing the course or the company. They should establish rapport by showing an ability to help but not be arrogant about it. It may require some subtle coaxing, but the sooner the group begins to participate the sooner they will appreciate the instructor's effort. The trainees may resent the instructor who tries to expose them openly before their peers, but they will be pleased with the instructor who allows them to make correct responses in front of their classmates.

PROGRAMING FOR THE RIGHT ANSWERS

With a little practice, instructors can program their teaching so that the group responds frequently and correctly. There is a small amount of information given, building up to an obvious conclusion. But the *students*, not the teacher, provide this conclusion. This works again and again, and the class is constantly involved. The sequence (oversimplified, of course) might go like this:

> **Instructor:** "The framus machine accepts only *round* gidgets. The rest are rejected, sent back for remelting and remolding. Now if this is the input (figure shown on the screen or drawn on the board) of the framus and a square gidget comes down this belt (indicate), what happens here? (point)"
> **Group (or individual student):** "It's rejected."
> **Instructor:** "Right! Now what happens to it?"
> **Group:** "It goes back to be remelted and remolded."
> **Instructor:** "O.K. Then where do you suppose it goes?"
> **Group:** "Back down the belt to the framus machine."

This little sequence demonstrates several points. It shows how the instructor can quickly get feedback to test a concept. It allows the group to be involved. It reinforces their answers with a rewarding "correct" evaluation from the instructor. Significantly, it doesn't take any more time than if the teacher were doing a straight lecture! Also, from the students' viewpoint, the time goes by much faster, and the material seems much simpler. The idea is simply to program the instruction so that the steps are small and the answers reasonably easy. Avoid long and involved answers; avoid complex answers too. Complexity may better be handled by the teacher, since the teacher should be more able to explain a complicated point than the group. Most any subject can be broken down to simple sequences such as the one just illustrated.

AVOID HIGH THREAT LEVELS

As has been said, trainees do not like to be embarrassed in front of their classmates. When instructors ridicule a trainee for saying the wrong thing, or for asking a seemingly simple question, they are probably building a dangerous "threat level." They may well be constructing an unnecessary barrier between the group and themselves. If the group gets the idea that the teacher is "looking down her nose" at them, they will make things difficult for her. Unfortunately, it is even possible for the students to misjudge an instructor for something she did that *seemed* like a threat, but was not intended as one. In other words, communication is always a problem, especially since the instructor may create unwanted attitudes by what she says or does.

Let us take a simple example and show some of the complications that may arise and what their solutions might be. In one hour, some 600 widgets can come through the line. In an effort to get class participation, the instructor asks, "How many widgets can come through the line in an hour?"

The question seems straightforward, but a student has been thinking in terms of *minutes*, so he answers quickly, "Ten!"

"Oh come on now! Just ten?" The instructor replies in astonishment, a tone of ridicule or disgust in her voice.

Someone else realizes a classmate is on the spot, and gives the correct answer. *But now the instructor is in trouble.* The class, realizing it is dangerous to say the wrong thing, becomes passive and probably would hesitate even to give the time of day at this point. The instructor, unaware of the situation she has caused, continues to ask questions but gets no response. She may even judge that the group is not very smart because they can't answer her questions. They won't answer, either, until they judge it is safe to stick their necks out.

How can the instructor avoid this threat level? By building up confidence, and giving the trainee a chance to correct his or her own error or develop the right answer.

"How many widgets can pass down the line in an hour?"

"Ten!"

Quick calculations tell the instructor that this is about a minute's output so she tries something to test the student.

"O.K., are you thinking of a *minute* or an *hour*?"

"Oh, yeah, you said an hour, didn't you. Let's see; that would be ten times sixty, or six hundred."

"Right! Now let's see what this would be . . . "

The small exchange was hardly noticeable, and certainly not embarrassing, since the trainee got a chance to correct his own error and explain why he made the mistake in the first place.

But suppose he had really been wrong? What if he had said the wrong number, and questioning brought out he thought ten was the number per hour? How can he be corrected without building up the threat level?

First, chances are that if one thinks this is the right answer, several others have the same misconception. More instruction may be needed. After all, the instructor has just gotten a good piece of *feedback*. In answer to a significant question, covering previous instruction, the trainee gave the *wrong* information. Somewhere, with one student or several, there has been a breakdown in communications. *The fault may very well lie with the instructor.* It would be an injustice to the whole group to assume that only one student does not know the correct response. An alert teacher would do a quick test to check on the class as a whole.

"How many widgets will pass down the line in an hour?"

"Ten!"

"O.K., is that in an hour or a minute?"

"An hour."

"How many of you say ten in an hour?" The instructor holds up her hand, indicating that a show of hands is desired. If several hands go up, the instructor knows that she must redevelop the idea. If no others go up, she goes back to the person answering incorrectly, but now asks the rest of the class for help.

"Let's look at it again. If there were ten in an hour, that would mean about six minutes to pass *one* down the line. Is that right?" The voice is pleasant.

"I don't know."

"Somebody else—what do you think?"

"It should be six hundred."

Since *that* student is obviously correct, the instructor can safely challenge him. "Why six hundred? That would be ten a minute!"

"Well, er, yeah, that's right. Ten per minute." The second student responds.

"How many say six hundred per hour?" The instructor asks, again asking for a show of hands. The majority raise their hands.

"All right, six hundred is correct, and let's see why. In a minute's time . . . "

The instructor has eased the embarrassment of the trainee who first answered incorrectly, and, by challenging the second trainee, redirected the attention from the first trainee to the second. Since the whole exchange was handled in a matter-of-fact way, no threat level should have developed. The first trainee may not answer again right away, but the rest of the group felt no real pressure. Later, if the instructor feels it necessary, she can ask the first trainee a simple question with an obvious answer (providing that trainee appears to be following the discussion), and give him a chance to redeem himself in front of the group.

These things may seem trivial to the uninitiated, but they are a part of the psychology of the classroom, and may have a large effect on the total success of an instructor.

WHAT ABOUT DISCIPLINE?

The unruly employee rarely appears in an adult class, but occasionally an immature or obnoxious employee shows up for a course. Dealing with such an individual was covered in detail in an earlier chapter, but since it may have an effect on the threat level in the class, it should be mentioned again.

The techniques for dealing with a quarrelsome, boisterous, or sullen trainee vary, of course, with each instructor and each group. *It is important to deal with such a person,* however, for the good of the group. Sometimes the group will deal with a person who is disrupting learning, and if the situation is solved, so much the better. But instructors shouldn't depend on the group to take care of the problem, nor should they wait for such an event. If immediate action is required, the first break for refreshments or lunch is the time to do it. If at all possible, the instructor should try to avoid a direct confrontation in front of the entire group. The conference should be private, straightforward, and friendly, but it should leave no doubt that the instructor is in firm control and will not sacrifice the rest of the group for the poor attitude of one person. Instructors should not resort to threats. Rather, they should simply state the fact. "Your attitude doesn't seem conducive to learning, and I don't want it to affect the rest of the group. Is there something I can help you with?"

Be alert to see whether this attitude represents that of the whole group or just that of the individual. The situation should not be built up out of proportion, and the instructor should sincerely try to solve any problems that are in the student's way.

Many problems of rowdiness in the classroom are brought on by the instructor's efforts to be a "regular fellow" and let the group have fun. Such a situation is dangerous, because when things get out of hand the instructor has lost the respect of the group and cannot restore order easily. Fortunately, though, problems requiring discipline are rare when the employees are away from the job and know someday they will be expected to use the material they have learned in class to further their own careers. Also, they know they are still employees and any improper action can be quickly reported back to their supervisors. However, instructors should *rarely* find themselves in situations so bad that they would have to threaten to report the employee.

INVITING THE STUDENTS BACK TO CLASS

In spite of all precautions, instructors will occasionally find themselves with a group of students who have mentally left them. The students have found the going dull, or are thinking of going home shortly, or are particularly uninterested in what's going on. For whatever reason, they aren't learning anything, and it becomes necessary to "invite them back to class." Unfortunately, it isn't as easy as saying, "Now pay attention; this is important." They've already decided it *isn't* important.

There are some techniques for doing this effectively. These have been mentioned in earlier chapters, but let's see how they work.

One is the "pick up the pencil" approach. The students will respond to such an invitation, and may have a moment of worry because they haven't been listening. What they are asked to write isn't so important just as long as it pertains to the subject under discussion. It may be that the instructor will ask them to develop a new idea, or reconstruct a concept already given. They may be asked to list some things which can later be used as discussion points. A variation of this idea (and a good one to use after lunch) is to have them work with a tablemate, or turn around and work in small groups. Now they have the benefit of movement, talk, and perhaps controversy.

Another method of inviting them back is almost a shock treatment. It is the "short quiz" approach.

"Take a piece of paper and answer these three questions."

The instructor purposely hasn't specified that they hand in the papers, nor that the papers be signed, although he or she may desire to do so. If this is done frequently, though, a pattern has been set. Whatever seems desirable for the subject at hand is all right. It may be that the best solution is for the students to exchange papers, coding their own instead of signing them, then for the instructor to go over the answers as a regular teaching activity. Answers can be gotten on a volunteer basis from the group. Papers can be circulated again for the trainees to take their own, or left at the front of the room for them to pick up later. The whole purpose is to rekindle interest that has been lost, perhaps because of faulty instruction. When the trainees are "back in the class," the instructor should make a more diligent effort to keep up their interest.

WHAT ABOUT HANDOUTS?

The question of what to do about handouts is always a big problem. Some instructors give the trainees everything needed at the beginning of the course. Some prefer to hand out material as it is discussed, while others wait until class is over to give out anything. The arguments for each seem valid in the context of the instruction.

Those who hand out everything first say that it avoids confusion during the training session, the material can be better organized ahead of time, and it saves valuable time that would be lost in circulating copies of the handouts. They also point out that the trainees get a better overall picture of the course by seeing everything in the beginning.

Instructors who prefer to hand out the material as they go argue that this places more emphasis on the material at a time when it is being talked about. Also, they say, it avoids confusion because there is no question about whether the trainee is looking at *the right thing at the right time*. It allows him or her to get things in the proper sequence, then see how the parts fit together.

The last group prefers to pass out the material after class is over so that the students' attention will be on the instructor, not the handout material. They say they prefer to cover the subject thoroughly during class, then give any material out later as further study or reference information.

Since these all appear to be valid arguments, *what is the right way*? This is like asking, "Which is the *best* kind of visual aid?" There is no *right* way, because each has advantages and disadvantages. Let's look at the problem from a different viewpoint and see if it is really as serious as it appears.

The obvious question to ask here is, "Why have handout material at all? What is the purpose—what are the trainees to do with it?" The same is true for *any material* (books, pamphlets, student's guides, etc.) given to the group. What is the purpose of such material? When does this fit into the learning process?

The students should be given a course guide or outline at the very beginning of the course. This will tell them where they are going and what they can expect to be talking about, and it will serve as a ready reference for checking on their progress. Other material can be given to them at the beginning of each class period or at the start of each day. This will serve to point out that particular session's activity. It will also avoid the confusion of passing out material during class. (Actually, little time need be lost even in passing out information at class time, unless there are large amounts of it. By counting out correct numbers of copies by rows or tables ahead of time, the instructor can do the job in just a few moments.)

If the material is not to be seen ahead of time (a situation which should be pretty rare), it still can be handed out at the appropriate time. The fallacy here is that one must wait to hand out everything because *one* or *two items* should not be seen prior to a particular teaching session. Where possible, put out as much material as possible ahead of time, to avoid doing it later. However, if much of the material is just "interesting reading matter" and not pertinent for class or nightwork, put it in a separate binder or folder so the trainees will not have to carry it with them all the time. Material that is to be used back on the job, but not during class, need only be given out the last day, or even mailed to the employees.

Some pertinent observations should be made here about several of the things mentioned so far. First, the idea that the students shouldn't have material ahead of time because they will read it instead of listening to the instructor is insulting to the teaching ability of the instructor. *If reading material is more interesting than a training session, then the teacher is at fault, not the procedure for handing out material.*

Next, material handed out just for "interesting reading" is likely to go unread. There is plenty of interesting reading available to employees back home without giving them more. If reading the material is a vital part of their learning requirements, then some kind of assignment should be given to make them read that material. If it is given for nightwork during the course, it shouldn't just be "busy work." Some accountability should be required, by either a short quiz or class discussion.

Another questionable practice is that of giving the students large quantities of material that is *already available back on the job*, such as copies from manuals or bulletins or house organs, or any other items that are normally kept as reference material on or near the job. The problem that arises is that the material given to the employees may become outdated, and if they are used to their own reference material, they may not realize that new material has come out. While the office copies are updated, theirs may stay as they got them from school, and they will then be using incorrect information. A way to avoid this is to give out *references* to material, rather than the material itself. That way the employees will use the proper source back on the job, and always have access to the latest information.

SHOULD THE STUDENTS TAKE NOTES?

Another question that almost always comes up is the matter of taking notes. How many notes should the students take? Does note-taking help or hinder learning? Will the students miss something while they are taking notes?

The answer to this is more clear-cut than the matter of handout material. The solution, in fact, is the answer to the question, "How well can people take notes?" The answer is that trainees vary considerably in their ability to record information in easily usable form. The instructor who leaves much of the learning up to note-taking runs the risk of losing valuable information. The inexperienced instructor may say, "You'd better take notes on this," and expect all the notes to contain exactly the same information.

The truth is, *most employees do not make much use of notes,* especially after they go back to the job. (This is different from college, where the students are in the same class for three or four months. There, of course, they make much more use of their notes.) If instructors feel notes are essential, they should devise a guide to see that the job is done correctly. An outline could be furnished, with ample blank space provided for additional writing. That way the student will already have the skeleton of the course, around which to build notes. The instructor can be reasonably sure that the trainees are writing the notes in proper sequence and about the right subject. If the notes aren't good, at least the outline will be of some help.

WATCH FOR FEEDBACK

One problem with requiring the trainees to take extensive notes is that it sometimes persuades the instructor that the trainee is getting the information *in writing, if not in his mind.* As a result, the instructor may make less effort to get feedback from the group for fear of disturbing their note-taking.

But there is no substitute for feedback.

Imagine standing behind a screen and directing an individual to put oddly-shaped pieces of wood together into some particular configuration. The task is almost impossible because there is no feedback on the progress being made. Has the individual got the pieces together correctly so far? Is the person ready for the next piece? Are any of the pieces upside down or backwards?

On the other hand, the task would be very simple if we could watch the individual putting the blocks together piece-by-piece. We would know when the instructions got confused, when a piece was crooked or reversed. We would know when the person was ready for the next piece. In other words, we would know exactly what the progress was *because we got immediate feedback each step of the way.*

Unfortunately, teaching is more like being behind the screen than watching the process step-by-step. We cannot watch pieces fall into place (or get turned around) in a student's mind. We cannot always tell from facial expressions, nor can we depend on questions from the group, because the group members may *think* they have everything straight. They may in reality have wrong information, incomplete information, or information that's out of order. In fact, the instructor may have given them the wrong information by mistake. Unless there is feedback, the instructor won't know this.

Feedback can be gotten by frequent short quizzes, hand-in assignments, oral recitals, or by the programming technique, in which the instructor allows the students to respond frequently. Feedback is more easily obtained where the threat level is low and the trainees feel free to ask questions. Questions provide good feedback information in themselves, and will do so as long as the instructor gives sufficient attention to the answers. *If the answer is more confusing than the statements that generated the questions, the trainees will soon learn to keep their mouths shut!*

WHAT ABOUT NIGHTWORK?

Often it is possible to reinforce learning with work to be done outside the class, probably at night. This is usually more satisfactory where "live-in" training is being conducted than when the employees return to their homes and families each night.

This nightwork can be beneficial in several ways. It can reinforce the day's activities. Depth problems or extensive reading can be done to reinforce and extend the activities of the class period. In addition, the assignment can include a preview of the next day's work. The out-of-class work may also turn up some questions that were not generated in class. The trainees may think they understood something the instructor did or said, but find that problems arise when they attempt the same thing on their own.

But there are drawbacks to nightwork.

Nightwork should not be just "busy work." It should be as meaningful and well thought out as the classwork. It should have a specific purpose to meet a specific objective. It should fit into the program easily, not in a strained or forced way.

If nightwork is given, and it is to be tedious or time-consuming, the day's activity should be reduced somewhat to allow for this extended work assignment. Employees who work hard in class all day do not make very good subjects for additional heavy learning assignments in the evening. The difficulty of the material will dictate the time limits, but on the average, *an early afternoon quitting time is ideal when extensive after-hours work is required.*

It is difficult to fit nightwork meaningfully into the day's activity. One solution is to give a night assignment that primarily reinforces the day's work, then goes into the next day's work in generalities. Each day, then, starts off with a review of the previous night's assignment with reference to the previous day's work. When all questions are cleared up, the new work begins. If possible, a few questions about the new assignment can be asked to get the class involved. Sometimes questions may be given the night before on the advance assignment. Thus interest is generated and the students will have had to give some accounting for their reading assignment.

Whatever use is made of nightwork, if the students were supposed to learn from it, *the instructor cannot assume they know it just because it was assigned.* The instructor must build in some means for feedback. If they aren't learning from it, the instructor will have to change it or drop it. They should not be made to do it just because everyone else has had to do it.

This is one more place in which objectives are critical, just as with any teaching technique. Whatever technique is used to improve learning in the classroom, the instructors should always ask themselves, "Is this the best way, under the present circumstances, to make it possible for the learner *to be able to do what I want him or her to do* when he or she leaves the class?

SYSTEMS OF INSTRUCTION

Before we talk about specific techniques of instruction, let's talk about some *systems* of instruction. By systems, we mean a format for using whatever technique we're involved in, whether it's a lecture, film, VTR, role play, or whatever. We've taken the liberty of creating some names, not to confuse, but to try to organize. To understand the names, and hence the systems, we need to make up some definitions of terms. First, there is what we'll call "input." This we are defining as new information, or a new conclusion, the first time it is introduced in the teaching situation. Next, there is what we'll call "output." This is "old" information or old conclusions, called old because they've been introduced before the teaching session. The first time a fact or a conclusion shows up, it's *input*. After that, it's *output*. It doesn't matter how the information got into the teaching session, whether by the teacher or the students, or by a film, or a book, or a programed textbook. If it's new, it's input; if it's recurring, it's output. It's as simple as that.

Direct Teacher-Input System

The simplest system, and the one most often used, is the *direct teacher-input system*. We immediately think of the lecture when we think of this system. It is the best example of the system at work. But there are other techniques within this system, namely, a film or other audio-visuals. Actually, a film is a direct input from the teaching source. So is a book or a cassette, since all of these fit our definition: input comes entirely from a teaching source. This includes all facts, examples, and conclusions.

INPUT ⟶ LEARNING ⟶ INPUT ⟶ LEARNING
(Teacher)   (Students)   (Teacher)   (Students)

But when we put films and slides and filmstrips and cassettes and video in this system, we will see how ineffectual they can be if we don't do something to get the students involved. In fact, when we're designing a program, and that program includes an audio-visual, we have to ask ourselves: "Do I want this to be only a direct teacher-input audio-visual, or do I want to use another system?" If it's not in this system, it's because we *planned* for it not to be. If we use this system, we have to remember that the learner is not giving us any feedback, so we can only hope the information is getting through. We have no evidence other than the frowns or smiles on the learner's faces and such evidence has proved unreliable in the past!

Teacher Modification System

As we go to a "higher" form of learning, the *teacher modification system,* we begin to get the students involved, and we begin to get some feedback on our teaching efforts. The process begins with a lecture, and all the *input* comes from the teacher or a teaching source. The instructor gives the students what is needed to comprehend the subject, then uses questioning of some form to get feedback. The feedback is *output,* since it's simply a repeat of what the teacher has said (or what has been shown in the film or read in the book). It is based on remembering what has been said and doesn't include any new conclusions or ideas. The teacher listens and decides if what is being said is what was really taught. If it is, then the teaching goes on to the next session. If not, there is a "modification" effort, which may be input or output.

INPUT ⟶ LEARNING ⟶ INPUT/ ⟶ LEARNING
(Teacher)   (Students)   OUTPUT   (Students)
                         (Teacher)

If the teacher merely repeats what has been said already, the modification is output. If the students heard the teacher wrong, it may be that by the teacher's repeating the same thing in different words, or the students rereading something they've already read, they will be able to see where they've missed the point of the lesson. On the other hand, the teacher may feel that *additional* information may be needed to clarify the problems the students are having understanding the subject. In this case, input will be used. A new approach, or a different insight, or new information may be given. Any input-type information must come from the teacher though, for it to stay in this system. The value of the system that involves output from the student over the direct teacher-input system is that it keeps the teacher informed on the location of the student's understanding, and allows the students to know how they stand. It can be used with the lecture, by going to questions-and-answers, and it can be used with films, video, etc., by having the students feed back what they have grasped from these aids. All it takes is a simple statement answering, "What was the suggestion in the filmstrip that would best solve this problem?" As the students give what they thought they saw, we're getting feedback. We modify it as necessary, and then go on to the next subject.

Student Discovery System

Perhaps the highest order of learning is where the students get all their own "Ah-ha's". Ideally, this can not only be a sure way of knowing that they will retain the information, but also a quicker way, as we'll see in the later part of this chapter. The skilled teacher—and it takes a skilled teacher to live comfortably with this system—knows just how much information to give to the learners so they can take it from there. The information, or problems, or questions are offered at a pace that's even with or just a little ahead of the learner, so the learner is able to keep up by application of the things learned, and by reaching out for new thoughts and ideas It's this reaching out that causes the learning experience to be valuable. When the learners have the information fed to them without doing more than just looking or listening, they aren't likely to be able to grasp the information or skill as quickly or as accurately as when they have to do a little work for it.

INPUT $\longrightarrow$ LEARNING $\longrightarrow$ INPUT/ $\longrightarrow$ LEARNING
(Teacher)   (Students)   OUTPUT   (Students)
                                  (Teacher)

An ideal situation, though admittedly one that is rarely found, is where the students are never told anything *they could tell the instructor.* If they have the information stored in the form of

experience, though maybe not organized, and find it easily, with
some direction, the instructor just sets the stage, points the way,
and lets the students go after the information. It's not a game,
though. The teacher doesn't bait the students, letting them try
to guess what is needed to solve a problem. It's a reasonably
controlled system, with both the students and the teacher knowing what the end, *desired* product is. The students know where
the information is to be found, and may already have some of it
stored away from past learning experiences. The best way to describe this method of teaching is to think of the teacher as a *fa-
cilitator of learning,* rather than as a *giver of information.* We're not
just talking about information exchange, either. Mostly we're
talking about *thinking.* We're talking about reaching a new set of
conclusions by a thought process that uses the information already given by the instructor, combined with information already obtained in past learning or experiences by the learner. It
may be no more than a bit of information given to the students,
then a question that enables the students to answer, "Oh, that
would be a case where we'd apply the principle we talked about
a while ago. . . ." (That's what we call letting the students get
the "Ah-ha's.") There's nothing spectacular about the system in
action. If somebody walked into the classroom and heard the
teacher talk, then stop and ask a question, it would be difficult
to tell whether to classify the system as teacher modification or
student discovery, because it would be necessary to know
whether or not the answers were coming as output or input. If
the question asks for an answer that comes from information
previously given, it would be feedback, or output, and would be
classified teacher modification. If the question required taking
previous information and working with it to come up with a
new conclusion, then it would be student discovery. *But just drop-
ping in and hearing the question and answer wouldn't tell us which system
was being used.* It isn't very spectacular, in other words, but the
student discovery system is very effective!

SELF-DIRECTED LEARNING

Before we begin to list various methods of instructing, let's talk
about a kind of instructing that could be called a system rather

than a method. The concept of students discovering the conclusions, as we have just talked about, isn't new in learning circles, of course. Back in the days when Socrates was asking questions to provoke thinking, he was hoping to get the learners to "discover" the answers for themselves. The idea of teaching machines and programed learning—relatively new in the world of supervisors—isn't that new as a concept, since it, too, is an effort to produce individual learning activities. However, while it isn't new, *it also isn't used very often.* It should be, but other means of teaching are easier, are less trouble, and have less risk involved.

It takes several considerations to gain skill at practicing techniques which allow students to discover things for themselves. Once we get into the habit, though, it's a very satisfying way to teach—and also makes very little strain on the instructor. There is preparation ahead of time. The effects of this, like most things we do in teaching, are directly proportional to the amount and quality of the preparation. What do we do in the preparation? We determine what the students should do to get to the place we want them to be at the end of the learning—after we've determined what the place is. We decide what is good for the learner to know, why it's good, and offer several means to learn it. (If possible, we let the learner decide which method to use to get there.) In reality, how does this work? Let's suppose we want the learners to learn how to use a new procedure. The procedure is spelled out in a manual which is available in the classroom. One way we could teach this procedure is simply to lecture on it, show pages from it on the overhead projector, have the class look up facts while we watched, and end up by asking, "Are there any questions?" We've done this for years, but haven't always been excited about the end results—when the students get back home and either don't use the manual or claim they can't find anything in it.

If we were using a self-directed learning approach, we would possibly eliminate the lecture and the overhead presentation. Instead, we would give them several situations where they would need the manual to solve the problems presented, then leave them on their own to find the solutions. We would offer help if they wanted some, but would not force ourselves on them. We would mention the available overheads, as well as other teaching aids, such as a series of slides or a video cassette, then give them a deadline for turning in a solution using the prescribed new procedures. We would leave it to them to let us know if they had problems, and to let us know when they were satisfied they knew how to find things in the manual. We perhaps would give then another situation—different from the last—when they finished the first one. Here again, they'd be on their own to find answers.

Many feel this takes too long, but actually, it nearly always gets the job done faster. There is no waiting by the faster students for the slower ones. There is no lock-step follow-the-leader teaching where everybody does the same thing at the same time whether they need to learn or not. We get to spend our time with those who need us, and we can move them along faster, if they need help. In one sense, therefore, everyone is not equal in the classroom. They do not all have equal learning ability; they don't have the same deficiencies; their interest isn't all the same; their encouragement from their supervisor back home on the job isn't the same. Because of this kind of inequity, we shouldn't feel we have to give everybody equal treatment. To reach a specified goal, we have to give different kinds of help to different people. Some will need more than others. The self-directed learning approach makes this easy to do, since we only have to help those who need help. Even then, we may simply direct them to a better source, or give them some alternative places to go for help, for example, to another student who is well able to help, to some teaching aid, or to a chapter in a book.

LEARNER CONTROLLED INSTRUCTION

Open Classroom

One of the most attractive forms of self-directed learning is what is called Learner Controlled Instruction (LCI) or the open classroom. This is a formal system of instruction that, contrary to the implication of the name, is a rather structured process. The structure is in the goal setting and in the measuring, and the contracting between teacher and student. In operation, there seems to be very little apparent structure, but in reality, there is. We won't try to give a complete analysis here, but we'll show some of the high points.

First, there is a set of goals or objectives. These may be constructed by the teacher, and added to by the student, or they may be a combination of goals where negotiation between teacher and student has settled on the need/advisability/capability of these particular ones. In other words, the teacher may develop a set of goals that can be met in a given period of time, or for which there are resources available. The students may ask for goals for which there are no immediate resources available for achieving them. These will be eliminated or changed enough to fit available resources.

After these goals are set, there is a discussion of how we will be able to tell when the goals have been met. This, too, may be negotiable. It may be in the form of some "product" the learner will prepare to show competency. It may be showing ability to make a certain grade on a written or oral test. It could even be on the word of the student that he or she feels the goals have been met. Once the decision is made, however, it is part of the "contract." The contract is negotiable at any time, of course, but it isn't expected to be changed much; certainly not often.

Once the goals and the goals' check have been decided upon, a learning map is developed. The instructor can prepare a set of instructional suggestions: lectures, books, audio-visuals, practical exercises, individual consultation, teaching machines, programed learning, or whatever else is available. The teacher can prepare theses with alternatives, or be rigid in certain requirements. The student is free to suggest other ways and build a "map" on his or her own. Once the learning process starts, the students may alter the map if other ways occur to them to reach the goal. After all, they know where they're trying to get to, so they should have some control over how they do it. But we should remember, once they've entered into the contract to reach a certain goal, they're supposed to make every diligent effort to get there. They can choose another map only when they can show that it will, in fact, help them reach the goal. When the students feel they have reached the goal, they present their products, or otherwise demonstrate they have reached the proficiency expected and agreed upon.

With this brief explanation, it may be difficult to grasp the overall effort of LCI, but at least it can be seen that there is some structure to it. Unlike learning efforts of earlier times, where permissiveness was the key, this system binds the students to certain goals and methods of getting there—unless they can find a better way. The students aren't free to do whatever they want to, whenever they want to, but they do have a chance to make any key suggestions and decisions about their direction. This is important, because one thing we know: particularly as learners get older, *we have to have their cooperation to teach them anything.*

TEACHING TECHNIQUES

We've talked about approaches to teaching and systems of instructing. Now let's look at some specific methods and techniques of teaching. We've talked about them in detail in a few instances, and barely mentioned them in others. Here we'll put several of them together and see their strong and weak points. Since all of them are used at one time or another by most trainers, we will not try to show the advantage of one over the other, but rather try to show the possibilities of each. In that way we can find out the best time to use each technique. Often, a very good method is used at the wrong time, to teach the wrong people or the wrong subject, and fails not because it's a bad technique, but because of the poor use of it. We'll try to give a little information about each technique to help avoid that situation. Since there are sources available on in-depth information on each of these methods of instruction, we will only summarize them briefly here.

Lecture

The most commonly used training method is the lecture. Of all the instructing done anywhere, the lecture makes up by far the greatest percentage of the teaching time. That is fairly natural, for the instructor has the information and the students don't, so what is more natural than for the instructor to tell the students what they should know? Basically, that's what a lecture is: telling. It may be in front of a large audience, behind an impressive speaker's stand, or it may be a relaxed session where the instructor sits on the edge of the table. In either case, the lecturer is giving out information—(*Note*: Even though it's *natural* and often used, it isn't necessarily the *right* technique to use all the time, as we'll see later.)

The advantages of the lecture are several. First, it's a quick way to present many words and ideas to a group of people. Size of the class is no obstacle. If the acoustics are good, the group may be as big as the room can hold. Since it's a one-way effort, the students don't have to have the facilities to speak back and be heard by the instructor. Timing is an easily controlled factor in the lecture, since the teacher has complete control over it. Lecturing is an easy way for a new instructor to get into teaching, and overcome stage fright. By lecturing behind a stand, there is both a feeling of security and some built-in authority. Notes can be placed on the stand, and even material that is being discussed for the first time isn't too frightening as the notes are readily available. The instructor can venture out from behind the stand, write on the board, show an object, even use the overhead, then return to the "safety" of the speaker's stand. Another advantage of the lecture is that it can be practiced ahead of time. The new—or even experienced—instructor can go over a point ahead of time, practice comments, try writing on the board or using the overhead, and by class time feel comfortable with the way his or her lecture sounds.

The disadvantage of the lecture is that it violates one of the very important learning requirements: involvement by the student is necessary for most retention. As we have said, the lecture is a one-way process, with the teacher depending upon the material or the presentation to capture the interest of the students. Often the students *see a show rather than a teaching effort.* This leads to good evaluations on the instructor's presentation, but is also often interpreted as good teaching. It may not be. Mainly, the absence of feedback is a distinct disadvantage. The instructor has no way of really knowing if the material is being received properly, hence has to guess if the students are getting all the facts and ideas being presented. A test may be given at the end of the lecturing effort, but there is little that can be done about those who don't get the information, since time is all gone. We might improve the next lecture for the next group, but it's too late for these students.

Lecture-Demonstration

We should make a distinction between the simple lecture, where the instructor stands up (or sits) and talks about the subject, and the situation where the instructor not only talks about the subject but uses some sort of demonstration. Technically, we think of a "demonstration" as showing some kind of equipment, or a model of a unit that has been scaled down for use in the classroom (or cut away for easy viewing). Actually, we can just as easily think of a demonstration as showing how something should be done, whether it's filling out a form on the overhead projector, or showing the proper way to speak to a customer on the telephone. It can be showing a video tape of a right and a wrong way to do an interview, in between lectures on the subject.

The advantage of the lecture-demonstration over the plain lecture is that it brings a touch of realism into the classroom, letting the students see what they'll actually be doing or working with. It also helps to build up interest. The students get a reprieve from just listening to lectures all the time; they may have to strain their necks, move around, and maybe even touch the equipment. The object is to make sure the demonstration is visible to all and is comprehensible. (Remember, we're still talking about all the information coming from the teacher. The students aren't involved in this method, as far as discussion is concerned.)

The disadvantage of the method of lecture-demonstration is that even though it does build some interest, it fails to get the students totally involved. They are more interested because they see a piece of equipment, hear and see it operate, and know the subject is real, but still they aren't carrying on any dialogue with the instructor. This lack of involvement often causes frustration in the learners. They're "so near, and yet so far."

Lecture-Discussion

The lecture-discussion finally gets the students involved. It is still primarily the instructor's show, but the students are being asked to express their opinions, and to answer questions, even ask questions. It may be that they're discussing things that have come up in the lecture, in response to the teacher's questions, or they may be reacting to the lecture-demonstration with questions about the equipment or the procedures.

The advantage of the lecture-discussion is that the students are now contributing to the learning process at work. They are helping the learning to take place, in other words. The instructor is getting feedback, so it's possible to know what the students are thinking, and how they are putting the pieces of information together. There is a break in the pattern, hence more interest and attention is apt to be paid to the lecturing.

The process is still controlled by the instructor though, and the lecture is still the prime activity in the classroom. The involvement by the students comes when the instructor is *ready for it*, not when the students are *needing it*. Here, again, we might get some frustration in students who know that they shouldn't talk too much, but who have found good results from the questions and discussions that have transpired so far. They're "nearer" but not quite there, as far as feeling a freedom of expression. In other words, there is involvement, there is feedback, but both are still limited to the time available between lectures.

Guided Discussion

As is obvious, we're moving increasingly toward more student participation. In the guided discussion, the lecture plays less of a part, and the instructor is doing more to facilitate learning than just giving out information. The advantages are that the students are now equal partners in the teaching-learning activity, and the teacher is getting a good deal of feedback. This technique is most often found in the student discovery system we talked about in the first part of this chapter. The instructor's role is one of carefully guiding the learners to conclusions, requiring them to think about the problem rather than giving them all the answers outright. The teacher still has control, but the controls are shared with the students, maybe just by a remark such as, "We should get this wrapped up in about half an hour."

There are some possible drawbacks to this technique, though. For one, it takes a skilled instructor to know the difference between a fruitful discussion and an interesting discussion where nothing is accomplished. A *"rap session" isn't a guided discussion.* But students aren't always good judges either, so they may become somewhat frustrated when they think nothing is happening, while actually the teacher feels that things are moving toward a worthwhile conclusion. On the other hand, students may "enjoy" a discussion on a topic that the instructor considers has no solution or no learning value, then be frustrated when the instructor calls a halt to the exercise. Creativity may be stifled to some extent but the decision to continue a discussion is left in the hands of the instructor.

Discussion Groups (Subgroups)

The final removal of strong instructor control is found when we go to a subgroup activity. The control is not on what each person contributes, but on the topic and the requirements of the exercise. The instructor may give the small groups a problem, some restrictions to follow, and the time limit for coming up with a solution, then leave them free. The trainer has control as far as the *overall* subject matter is concerned, but not on the discussion in the small groups. The more specific the instructions, however, the more limited is the discussion in the groups.

The advantages of this kind of technique is that it places the accountability for the end product squarely on the shoulders of the members of the subgroups. They have a topic and they have a deadline. Each group is working separately on the same problem (usually), so although there is freedom to use initiative and imagination, the purpose and learning objectives are under control. Another advantage is that this method allows the students to become much more involved than they would be if the class was all together in an exercise. It's possible to have many people talking at the same time, and all of it constructive for they are looking for solutions. At the same time, they're building some commitment and will be quite interested when the groups assemble into one classroom at the end of this part of the exercise.

In a way, this is also a cause of one of the disadvantages. This commitment to one of the solutions, which may be shared, compromised, or dismissed altogether, may prevent the students from becoming committed to the final solution. A good instructor can work out the compromise easily enough, but the inexperienced one may not be able to. Another drawback with this method is that the very lack of control may allow one or more of the subgroups to get on the wrong track and waste valuable time before turning in the right direction again. The skillful trainer always listens carefully (though perhaps without the students knowing it) to see if the discussion is going in the right direction. When it's obvious that a group is having trouble, the instructor may have to move in and give more specific directions. If this isn't done constructively, the group may resent it, but if it is done properly, the group will appreciate not wasting any more time.

Simulation

We're going to talk about simulation in a very broad way, calling almost every thing that looks like the job, "simulation." There are all kinds of simulation, such as, for example, simulating a telephone call from a customer. In this section, we're saying that anything that makes an effort to look like the job, sound like the job, feel like the job, etc., is simulation. There are some specific training activities that in themselves have names, and we'll talk about each of these briefly. Again, there is much available on all of them, so we'll only summarize here.

Simulation: In-basket

The "in-basket" exercise is a device used to train people who will be looking at letters, memos, and notes, and making decisions as a result. It is designed to appear to be a typical in-basket that might be on the desk of someone who is new to the job. The situation usually calls for a person to have an hour to catch a plane or attend a meeting, to be alone, unable to contact anyone, and to be looking at a set of 20-25 pieces of paper left over from the previous occupant of the desk now being used. "You have this job now and must react to the items in the in-basket. You have an organizational chart, a calendar, and a brief description of the operation." With these instructions the participant launches into the pile of papers, free to proceed in any manner desired. As it turns out, the in-basket is not just a random set of letters and notes, but rather a carefully worked out, integrated, interrelated set of documents which can test and train on a number of different managerial skills.

The advantage of the in-basket is that it touches reality. The items are things that could happen. To get through, the person has to make a number of decisions—or postpone them—and it is from these decisions, or postponements, that the observation and training come in. The learning takes place *after* the exercise is completed, from the discussion, subgroup activity, or instructor inputs. Because it is timed, pressure is present, which aids the realism. The in-basket can test and train for such things as organization, decision making, problem solving, perception, sensitivity, and planning. Its versatility makes it a valuable training tool.

One of the chief drawbacks to using the in-basket is that the trainees do not have to live with their decisions, as they do in real life. One can only predict the outcome of the decisions, not experience them in any way. Another problem is that because they *look* like ordinary letters and memos, many instructors try to make up their own exercises without knowing the intricacies with which a successful in-basket is filled.

Simulation: Case Study

For many years now the case study has been the mainstay of many supervisory and management training programs, as well as programs in other fields, even clerical and sales training. The case study can be as simple as a one-sentence description of a situation, and as complicated as a folder full of information and an accompanying film or video presentation. In whatever form, though, the purpose is the same: create a situation with a problem and let the participants work on possible solutions. If the case study is designed well, it will be possible for "wrong thinking" people to get "wrong answers." In other words, the best solution isn't always obvious. If the person reading the case is naturally an autocratic manager he will find information condoning this approach. Other information would refute this approach, once it's pointed out, of course. Generally, the participants work on the cases individually, then get together in small groups and try to develop solutions together. These are then presented before the entire group and a general discussion is held.

The advantages of the case study are many. It is realistic; it is interesting; it is fairly easy to prepare; it can teach many different aspects of the job; it allows for much involvement; it provokes much discussion; it causes the students to have to deal with real problems; it fits almost any kind of situation; and it provides easily for role play and follow-up on answers that are given. With these advantages, it is easy to see why it is such a popular training technique.

There are drawbacks, though. One is that while case studies are easy to prepare, some people tend to prepare them without removing the obvious answers, or without asking good questions. ("What can be done to prevent Agnes from becoming upset over the decision to move her to another location" is asked when, in reality, it's determining that Agnes will be upset that should be the goal. "What are going to be some of the consequences of this decision?" would be a better question.) Another problem is that the students still don't have to live with their decisions. If they decide to call Agnes in and talk to her, they don't have to live with that action—unless the instructor goes into a role play situation right away. Another handicap is that if the problem is too complex, there may not seem to be an answer to the situation, and the students may go away from the exercise asking, "But what should I do in a situation like that?" Instructors may tend not to give answers to cases, saying that there is often more than one solution. They should at least suggest some right and wrong possibilities.

Simulation: Action Maze

This is a step beyond the case study and is harder to prepare. The action maze consists of a problem and some suggested solutions, and the participants chose one solution for their answer. This choice leads them to another stage where they are told what happens when this decision is made, some more information is given, some more choices are given, and the process continues. After a while the students come to a final solution. The work can be done in teams or individually. Points can be given for rapid movement, or for the least number of choices.

The advantage of the action maze first of all is that the students have to live with their decisions. They see what happens when they decide to take a certain course of action. Interest is always high, and when the students are working in a group, much learning can take place as the group argues out the possible decisions to make, and the consequences of each. In addition, since the action maze is an extension of the case study, it has the same advantages of this technique.

The disadvantages are mostly matters of the complexity and difficulty of preparing the action maze. Providing the right choices and the right actions for each choice takes a great deal of skill, or it can lead to false learning. Time is another factor. The action maze takes much longer to go through in the classroom than the case study, and there has to be a measure of just how much the particular learning from this exercise is worth. Also, sometimes the students get lost in the maze, forgetting what decisions they have made, and even why they made them. If the maze is improperly constructed, it may be interesting for the students but may teach little or nothing worthwhile.

Simulation: Incident Process (Critical Incident)

The incident process, or critical incident as it is sometimes called, is a combination of the regular role play and the action maze, except it doesn't give the students the choices; they have to ask questions on their own in order to get more information. If they do not ask a question on a particular subject, they may be using old information (which should be obvious to them) or they may operate on biases or assumptions—all of which is very life-like. Typically, the students would be broken into subgroups, given the short incident along with an understanding of the procedures, and they would begin to try to solve the problem. It might be a production problem, an absenteeism, or an interpersonal problem. Each subgroup would decide if it needed additional information, and if so, what is needed in what priorities. The subgroups would find out from one of the instructors, be charged with a question, and would go back to work on the additional information and the next question they would ask. Each group does the same until one of them comes up with a question which is, in fact, the solution to the problem. Again, the scoring can be measured against time, and/or number of questions asked.

The advantage of this approach is that the students are in a more life-like situation than any of the other methods mentioned, since in real life they have to make decisions and live with them, but they do not get alternatives already available to them. In the incident process, they must decide which questions will give them the best view of the problem, and also when to stop getting more information and start working out the problem.

The difficulty with this technique—in addition to the inherent complexity—is that it can become unwieldy for one instructor, and when there is more than one, there is a problem of everybody giving the same, *consistent* answers. Since there is no restriction on what questions can be asked about any phase of the problem, there is no way to prepare for all the questions that might be asked. In the rush of working on the problem there is no way to record all the content of the questions being asked, so a good memory serves well.

Simulation: Games

The most sophisticated form of simulation is the game, usually called management games. Many use the computer to move things along more quickly and to allow the students to engage in decision making rather than computing. The typical situation is the running of a company over a period of several quarters, making decisions on marketing, expansion, pricing, stockpiling, etc. These decisions are made in subgroup teams, and the teams compete over the period of the game. The results are calculated as to the effect of the decisions on the next quarter of operation and other decisions are made from these results. Depending upon the complexity of the game, the answers can be given to the teams either within a few minutes or up to a day or so. The winner is usually the team showing the most amount of net savings or net profit.

The advantage is again the living with decisions, but more so here in that the decisions affect the whole company, rather than just one small operation. Because there are a number of variables, the students are able to see how one decision on one area can influence the rest. It also allows them to see that there often isn't one correct answer, but sometimes compromises are valuable and even correct. Because the students learn to see how decisions on different parts of the business must interrelate, this is a good method for creating a better understanding of other people in the business.

One disadvantage of the game is that it invariably must deal with the more tangible things of the business world, things like money, material, resources, taxes, and so on, and cannot deal effectively with the "people" aspects of doing the job. There's no way in a management game that attitudes can be dealt with adequately, or morale, or poor supervision. Since it's often difficult to quantify these things, they're not figured into the games. Time is another factor. It takes time to do the computations, and that ties up the students for long periods of time while they make their decisions. Reporting and recording and figuring the results of the decisions also takes time, and so other things must be taught in the meantime. Of course, for the most part, these types of games are generally used at middle and higher levels of management (though not restricted to this use), and the time can be well spent in related financial or organizational problem areas.

Simulation: Role Play

The role play has been around for many years, and comes in and out of favor. The reason for its popularity is that it's usually fun to do, and most people remember what they said and did during a role play. Some will object, saying that people rarely play the role they play in real life, or they play a role they wish they could play but probably won't in real situations. Studies are inconclusive on this point, for the most part. The technique is simply one of somebody playing a role of the person to be talked about: a customer, a clerk, a subordinate, a disgruntled employee—anybody we want to learn to deal with. There are all kinds of combinations. The instructor can play one role, pick a student for another, and they can go through a role play in front of the class. There can be a "doubling" effect, where the instructor plays one role, and anyone in the class can pick up and play the other role as he or she feels like it. The role passes around through the class. Two students (or three or four, as the roles are required) can play while the others watch, or there can be multiple role playing going on, where the class is broken up into small groups with each one engaged in the same role play.

The advantages of the role play are obvious: participation in a real-life situation, personal involvement, a chance to experiment with an approach to dealing with people, a chance to observe others playing a role that we might be interested in playing ourselves, and all this in a safe environment. If the teacher plays one of the roles, there is the additional chance for him or her to structure the activity to bring out particular problems in interpersonal relations or sales effort.

The disadvantages are also several in number. First, there is the problem of realism. It is a "role" and many never let themselves go into a real-life performance. Also, since it is role playing, many people tend to get into the dramatics, *rather than the learning.* This is especially true of some instructors. They like the technique so much they become actors instead of trainers, and go into the role with a flourish. Equally bad, they will go into great fanfare to set the stage, bring in props and backdrops to create an office, when all that would be needed would be to say, "Okay, this is my office and you've just walked in with this complaint," and let the imagination do the rest. We need to draw the attention to the words and the effect of the words, not the actions that produced the words. (This is one area that video has affected: people watch the *acting,* instead of listening to the dialogue.) Finally, one drawback to the role play is that often it takes a long time to make a minor point, and sometimes the point is missed altogether. It takes a skilled *instructor,* not a skilled actor, to make role playing successful!

Computer Assisted Instruction

Many years ago people in the education field were working with teaching machines as a device to interact and react directly with students. The idea was to have students answer some question posed by the machine (usually in written form) and get as quick a response as possible on correctness. In their more sophisticated form the machines recorded attempts at answers, even wrong answers. They frequently gave rewards for correct answers or for minimum attempts to get correct answers, and sometimes they even gave tangible reinforcement in the form of prizes or candy.

There were all kinds of problems with this approach, mostly with cost, size, and keeping the reaction time to a minimum. However, they worked, people learned from them, and we learned a lot about how people learn. For the most part, programed instruction (which we'll talk about in another chapter) was a direct result of teaching machines, being the "software" that was fed into the machines. As has always been true, the machines were no better than the people who put the information into them, and the programs or software could do only what the programers were able to build into the teaching-learning modules. What was needed was something that had more flexibility, was easier to operate, and had much less reaction time. That "something" turned out to be the computer.

When computer technology got to the point that it could respond to simple language and could be programed to give almost limitless flexibility and variety of answers (and choices of answers), the conversion from teaching machines to computers was an easy step. The result was Computer Assisted Instruction, CAI as it is usually called. Like most things in instruction, it isn't a panacea, but it is very effective in doing what teaching machines started out to do. It allows the student to "converse" with it and will respond to an answer immediately. It will allow the student to progress in a linear fashion or it will lead the student through any number of branches, sidetracks, loops and even bypasses. Students can control their own pace, enter at various points in the program, repeat themselves, and redo a section. They can be tested and graded, and they can measure their progress with great accuracy. As with all techniques, it has its drawbacks.

Unless the computer is being used by a very large number of students or is used primarily for other purposes in the organization, the cost quickly becomes prohibitive. The cost includes more than the computer itself; there is the time and cost of the programing expertise, the computer time in validation, the usage time charged against the computer, the communication lines between terminals (if there is remote access required), the program upkeep (keeping the program current), and other costs which aren't as different from traditional training techniques. Another important consideration and disadvantage is the difficulty of either training a computer operator in both the subject and the teaching-learning knowledge any good trainer needs, or teaching a good trainer to program the computer. Both are time consuming, and we rarely get a perfect match in skills and knowledge of all three aspects (training, programing, and subject knowledge).

Interactive Video

It may be that the world is now converted to gathering more knowledge from the video tube than from any other single source. People may be *exposed* to more time with other techniques, but they may not be ready to learn as quickly and patiently with the traditional techniques as with the TV set. Be this true or false, there is little doubt that the present-day learners are growing to maturity with many hours of watching television, hence they will more likely respond easily to teaching efforts that make use of video. Enter "Interactive Video." As the name reveals, the learning process is one in which the learner interacts with a form of television. There are different ways in which this happens, and there will be others as the computer and television technology link up more and more. The basic idea is similar to CAI; students look at a screen and react to things that happen on that screen. As we say, "The possibilities and opportunities for the instructors and the learners are limitless."

An obvious advantage is the ability to do student-centered instructing, using self-pacing, built-in films, paperwork, and preprograming of any kind, as with the computer. The screen serves as the classroom; the student teaches on a self-need basis with the same branching capabilities mentioned earlier, and can go through anything from forms and reports to psycho-motor skills. Further, if the program is tested well enough, there is the guarantee that all the learners who take the program will get the same thing, wherever and whenever they take it. With the addition of case studies and vignettes the learner can interact with paper exercises; or in subgroups an action maze or roleplaying can make the learning experience even more valid.

The disadvantage is that interactive video suffers from the same ill that most other training techniques do, especially those that are self-directed. It is no better than the designer can make it. The students have little chance to improve on what's been put into the design and can get no more out of it than has been put into it. If the designer used imagination, plenty of resources, and good learning expertise, the programs will reflect this. If not, the program will be dull, routine, and noncaptivating, and the learner will flounder in the self-pacing activity. There is also the cost factor mentioned in the discussion of CAI, though in this case there is probably less risk of getting into a rapidly accelerating cost figure. If good audio visuals already exist in the organization, they can be used to keep the cost down. Programs can be produced in-house with minimum studio facilities. Another drawback to this technique is the lack of expertise in designing effective learning activities. As with CAI, there may be no one person who has the video knowledge, the subject knowledge, and the training knowledge; so it may take a team rather than only one person. This of course affects the cost.

Miscellaneous Techniques

There are other techniques, ranging from fishbowling, to hypnosis, to brainstorming that require special skills and are used only in special situations. There are panels and conferences and symposiums, but these generally make use of the techniques we've been talking about. Here we have talked about the techniques most often used by most trainers. With a little effort and thought, the skilled instructor can find a method that's just right for the subject and for the students being taught. Any technique is only as good as the user, and no one method is perfect for all kinds of teaching. We have to weigh the advantages and disadvantages carefully, see what we're gaining and what we're giving up with each technique we use. If we try a new method, we may feel a little awkward at first. We shouldn't let this discourage us since we're learning a new skill. If we're using the best technique, after a while we'll begin to feel comfortable with it and see the good results from our efforts.

Exercises and Questions

1. *Without* breaking the class into groups, discuss the following question: "What is the best technique to use in getting students involved during the teaching-learning situation?

2. Dividing the class in subgroups of three or four, come up with an answer to the following question. "How is it possible to 'force' students to become involved even if they prefer not to be?" Report this information to the entire group and see whether all can agree on the subgroup solutions.

3. Now answer the following questions relative to Questions 1 and 2. Which of two methods got the most *total* participation, i.e., the most people talking? Which method got the most people involved in working for an answer? In which did the instructor work the most?

4. Discussion questions: How can involvement techniques serve to measure whether or not objectives are being met? Is it possible that we can imitate a technique exactly and still not be as effective as the person we are imitating? (Give examples.)

chapter 15
LEARNING THEORY AND THE INSTRUCTOR

It seems well not to add to the lengthy discussions of various learning theories that are already a part of our literature. Much controversy exists, and to some extent it has probably been helpful in producing the information now available. Certainly it would be unlikely that the supervisor who has been asked to become a teacher need ever get embroiled in a controversy over learning theories. The supervisor as a teacher is more interested in *what* works than *why* it works. In this chapter we will discuss some things that *help* learning and *hurt* learning. This should be of prime interest to the instructor.

REPEAT, REPEAT, REPEAT?

For a long time it was thought that the best way to learn was by repetition. Now it is generally agreed that mere repetition, without any involvement, is not the most efficient way to learn. The students will retain the information longer if they somehow get involved in working out the solution, or are rewarded for doing a thing right. This does not mean that repetition or drill does not help; it means that the trainees need to get involved to the extent that they understand what is going on. For instance, if employees are to learn to operate a machine, they are more likely to remember how if they know what is going on at each step. Compare the two methods below:

1. "Push the far right-hand button. Pull the yellow handle until a high-pitched squeal is heard. Release the yellow

lever immediately. Push the green lever and push the far left-hand button at the same time. When a thump is heard, release them both. Push the center button one time . . . "

2. "Push the far right-hand button to turn the winch on. Pull the yellow handle to start the lift arms. When they reach the top and can go no further, a high-pitched 'squeal' will be heard. This means the arms are straining against the top of the lift. Release the yellow handle immediately to prevent undue strain on the arms. The far left-hand button is a safety button that releases the green lever. The green lever starts the winch line moving in. Press the button and push the lever at the same time. When the line hook is completely wound in, there will be a 'thump' as it hits the windlass. Release the green lever and the far-left button. The green lever is now locked in place. Press the center button to turn the winch off."

The idea is that, in (1) repetition of the steps will produce learning, but the explanation in (2) of what is happening will enable the operator to learn and *retain* the information better. Drill is still required, but because the operator knows what the squeal and thump are, the drill is more meaningful.

PRACTICE MAKES PERFECT?

The old adage about practice is almost, if not completely, true. One grave danger is that the practice may include errors; that is, *it may not be directed toward perfection.* The employee may be practicing some *wrong* actions along with the proper ones.

For instance, suppose that a student learning about finance or economics is practicing changing money value from Present Worth to Future Worth. He uses the correct interest figure but the wrong conversion formula. If he repeats this on enough problems before finding out he is wrong, he may become proficient in solving the problems *incorrectly.* In this case practice makes imperfect! Here again is the need for *feedback.* Both the instructor and the trainee could have stopped the error if there had been feedback soon enough.

Another consideration about practice is that, for a given amount of it, *the student learns better if the practice time is spread out over extended intervals.* Two hours of practice would generally result in better learning and recall if done in four 30-minute sessions than in one straight two-hour session (unless the operation required the full two hours to complete).

This means that when the instructors introduce to a group a subject that requires repetition in order for the student to gain the necessary skill, they should think seriously about building in later practice sessions. Instead of just devoting a long class period to practice, they may want to schedule some practice in class, then make an out-of-hours assignment for more practice, and perhaps use some time the next day in a final check-out. Since the "forgetting rate" is highest immediately after learning, the instructors may require additional practice sessions soon after the training program is over. They should be sure, of course, that the students know they are practicing correctly.

STUDENTS SHOULD PRACTICE

Much of what we call practice, or repetition, actually consists of the *instructor* repeating things in front of an inactive class. The *trainees* should perform the repetition, the practice; *they* should be saying the key phrases; *they* should be repeating the proper steps. Again, there is the need for active participation. The instructor asks the question; the students respond with the answer. They are not passively uninvolved, but *actively involved in saying or doing the things they will need to say or do back on the job.*

Teachers of public speaking often say, "Tell them what you're going to tell them, then tell them, then tell them what you've told them." That technique has a definite place, but that place is *not* the classroom. It would be better to say, "Tell them what you want them to tell you, let them tell you, then let them tell you what they've told you."

STUDENTS DIFFER

Because there are so many variables involved, it is difficult to lay down firm rules for the instructor to follow in the classroom.

The major variable is, of course, the student. No two are alike; no two come with identical backgrounds of education and experience. Even if they did, their ability and capacity to learn would be different, so they still could not be treated the same. Some already have the foundation for a subject; some lack it, but grasp things so rapidly that they present no real problem; others lack the background and learn slowly.

If the instructor has trainees with all of these backgrounds and qualities in the same classroom at the same time, she may have an insurmountable problem. She may simply decide to aim for the good of the most people—and the company—and start out. The lowest and highest achievers will suffer the most. Outside help will benefit the slower learner, and additional challenge will keep the fast learner interested, but at best the wide variation is an unfortunate handicap to the instructor.

THE STUDENT'S NEED TO KNOW

One of the strongest factors influencing the trainees is their need to know when they are right. Short quizzes will give them important feedback, because they can check their thinking and action against the correct answers. Nothing seems to motivate people more than being right, so students who succeed *and know it* will be motivated to repeat their success.

The alert instructor will give all the students ample opportunities to find out that they are right, and various ways of doing this have been discussed in earlier chapters. Not only frequent short tests but even longer tests over entire units will help the students know where they stand and whether what they are doing is correct. Allowing the class to come up with an obvious conclusion gives them feedback and reinforcement on a correct method of solving a problem. Writing *their* answers on the board allows them to see and know the results, and keeps them involved.

FROM KNOWN TO UNKNOWN

People learn new information best when it is developed from information already known and accepted by them. *The way to arrive at facts not previously known is by way of facts already established.* Forcing the trainees to "unlearn" things they have accepted for some time is a difficult way to teach. While it is necessary occasionally, it should be avoided if possible. One way to keep from "losing" students is to teach the new way without confronting them with the necessity of forgetting about the old way.

The instructor who comes in and says "I know you've all been doing this a certain way, but you can just forget that because I'm going to show you another way," is really inviting rebellion in the minds of the trainees. He would do better to lead them along, *with their participation,* to a correct solution based on what they know, but with a newer approach. After they have practiced the new method and feel at ease with it, they will be less interested in holding on to the old way. The emphasis should be on doing the job *better—not differently.*

RELATE FACTS TO IDEAS

Another concept in going from the known to the unknown is to relate the new *facts* to a known *idea.* The idea may not even be related to facts themselves. The Parables were good examples of this.

For instance, a switching system that scans many different inputs might be described as "a champion chess player with many chess boards around him. He moves from one board to the next and remembers how the board looked the last time he saw it. If there have been any changes, he knows he must do something; if not, he moves to the next board. The scanner in the switching system *is like the champion* who moves from one board to the next. The memory store *is like the mind* of the champion . . . "

By relating new information to something that is familiar to them, the students can grasp even a complex switching system fairly easily. The chess player has no real relation to the switching system, but he provides a convenient handle to tie the facts to. The alternative would be to describe the parts without relating them to anything familiar to the trainees, "The scanner does thus and so; the memory store performs this or that function."

Pity the poor employees who are confronted with an instructor who reads or states fact after fact with no tie-in to anything familiar. While the students' minds wander, completely unable to retain or understand the facts, the instructor quotes statistics, then facts about the statistics, then figures to back up the facts behind the statistics. Even the prolific note-takers are lost because they see no particular organization to the flood of facts. Soon all they have is a page full of incomprehensible information. The instructor *might* have said, "Picture a large pie cut down the middle. One half represents the amount spent for salaries last year. The other half is the overhead, profit, etc. Now cut this last piece into three equal parts . . ." With this picture in mind the students can draw their own visuals. They have an easy figure to tie the facts to and are much more likely to grasp (and remember) the information being taught.

A PLACE FOR EVERYTHING

None of us likes "loose" facts, facts that don't seem to belong anywhere. Just as people learn better when facts relate to something familiar, they also learn better when the facts *relate to each other.* That is why information is usually presented step-by-step, so that every part relates to the whole and to each of the other parts.

Poorly organized material can cause the instructor to present facts out of sequence or in an unrelated manner. The resulting learning will most likely be a disappointment. We understand this in teaching children, but we forget that the principle applies to adults as well. The child who easily learns to count "5, 10, 15, 20 . . . " would have difficulty in learning a sequence such as "3, 17, 10, 13 . . . " The employee who is now a student finds equal difficulty in learning a lot of unrelated facts such as "15,000 rpm, designed by Acme, 152 salesmen, $5.83 for the replacement clutch . . . "

TOO MANY WORDS SPOIL THE . . .

We have seen that words are codes by which we transmit facts, concepts, ideas, etc. Without more feedback than is generally available in the classroom, it is difficult to know when the message has been "decoded" correctly. To overcome this handicap the instructor may continue to send more of the same code (in other words, keep talking). Ideally, he should cut off when the message has been understood. But this is rarely the case; he may cut off too soon, or he may go on talking after the correct learning has taken place.

Cutting off too soon is obviously frustrating to the student. They are, in effect, left standing on the threshold of understanding with the door closed in their faces. Feedback will tell the instructor when he has stopped teaching too soon. If the trainees are lucky, he will have another chance to fill in the gap for them.

But what if the instructor talks too much? Unfortunately, normal feedback will not help here. There is no way of knowing just when "the light dawned" for the student. There is evidence to show that the students get as frustrated when the instructor talks beyond the learning point as when she stops short. Further, the things the instructor says beyond the point of first understanding may even *confuse* the students, since they will not be listening or concentrating as well from that point on.

Another difficulty here is that the instructor can be pretty dogmatic about how much the trainees should hear and just how much they need to hear before they can understand a subject. Instructors may even ignore feedback which gives positive evidence of correct learning because they have prepared a longer

lecture, and "know they couldn't understand this quickly." Good instructors should be just as willing to stop early as to work overtime. After all, it's learning they're looking for, and when it takes place, their work has been accomplished.

WHAT IS LEARNING?

Psychologists cannot explain exactly what happens when learning takes place. There are theories, of course, and much research is being done. One thing is certain: learning is a change within the individual, not something that is "done to him." In the classroom, the instructors do not *transmit* learning. In a sense they actually do not *teach* the student, although the expression is all right when understood in context. Whatever happens, the student controls the results. Teachers provide the classroom environment, the facts, the stimuli, perhaps even the motivation, but learning takes place within the student's mind.

The point of all this is that instructors sometimes feel that because they have provided an ideal learning situation, learning has taken place. Such may not be the case. The instructor who is amazed when an employee doesn't know something and blurts out "but don't you remember—I *told* you . . . " demonstrates that she doesn't realize that *telling* is not *teaching*. For classroom definition at least, learning takes place when the student gets involved enough to readjust what he already knows and can do to include the new information, the new skill. Anything short of this is not satisfactory learning, hence not satisfactory teaching, especially if all or most of the students fall short of this objective.

Exercises and Questions

1. (This is an exercise to see just how much—or how little—we know about "learning theory.") Dividing the class into subgroups, see which group can come up with the longest list of facts (?) about learning. Use clichés, traditions, or known facts. Do not quarrel about their correctness, just write them down. Next combine the lists and put the items on the board (abbreviate). Discuss the list from the standpoint of whether or not we really know very much.

2. Looking at the list, have the groups vote by show of hands on how many agree or disagree with the statements. If we know so little, and can't always agree on that, how can we ever become good instructors?

3. One of the most significant things we know about learning is that we are able to better retain those new words or concepts which we can associate with facts we already know. If the instructor says "tree" or "cow" we are better able to get a picture than if he says "ferromagnetic domain." Is this ability or lack of ability to associate a new concept with known facts the criterion that makes a subject "easy" or "hard"? How could the subject "tree" or "cow" be difficult? How could "ferromagnetic domain" be easy?

chapter 16
THE USE OF PROGRAMED INSTRUCTION

Programed instruction is much like learning theory in that it is risky just to try to trace its history. Even defining it is bound to offend someone. Regardless of its history or the controversy surrounding it, programed instruction (or programed learning) is a part of the total training technology. Fortunately, it is not necessary for the instructor or the student to know where it came from to use it successfully!

WHAT IS PROGRAMED INSTRUCTION?

Programed instruction (or PI) is a technology in which the trainees are essentially on their own to learn a predetermined skill or bit of factual information. The material is generally presented so that they can go through it without the assistance of an instructor. A teacher may be available, but essentially it is a self-instructional procedure. There are different kinds and methods of programing but all of them require some kind of frequent response from the participant. Usually the participants read or look at information which directs them to fill in a blank or select an answer. The program is so constructed that they should make the correct response almost 100% of the time.

Some programs require discrimination, but "ease" the student into discrimination by making the correct choices very obvious in the beginning and increasing the difficulty as the student becomes more proficient (or learns more). Other programs require only a response and no discrimination. The student is prompted openly or subtly ahead of time, then responds to a question on the prompted information. There are many variations and combinations of programs and most trainers are familiar with some form of programs. In programed instruction, learning is constant and time is the variable; in classroom instruction, time is constant and *learning is the variable.*

The important thing to remember is that *a good program teaches.* Not only that, but it teaches a specific thing. It is possible to know, with reasonable certainty, exactly what the learners will be able to do when they finish the program. The program will specify this in its objectives. In fact, part of the definition of programed instruction should include the use of *realistic objectives built around an accurate task analysis.* (Since many books and articles on PI are available, we will not discuss what it is any further, only how it can be used effectively by the instructor.)

WHAT ARE THE ADVANTAGES OF PI?

Because the objectives of PI are spelled out in specific terms, the instructor can know exactly where the trainees will be when they have finished a program. Such a condition does not always exist with classroom teaching. Most commercial programs come to the instructor already validated (and should include the validation information). The instructor can tell who the program is designed for and what performance can be expected from those taking the program.

Another advantage is the fact that the program is an individual assignment, and no trainee need wait for another before proceeding. Each learns at his or her own best pace, without being hindered by slower or faster learners.

Still another advantage is the cost. Although the initial cost may seem high (because it usually is out-of-pocket and a large one-time expense), subsequent copies include only the cost of publishing. When it is considered that the instructor is buying a reasonably assured result, the cost is insignificant. This is especially true because the *same* result can be obtained over and over again, something that is sometimes difficult with different instructors or even with the same instructor at different times.

There are other advantages, but these are enough to make PI attractive to a teacher.

WHAT ARE THE DISADVANTAGES?

Some of the advantages turn into disadvantages when the programs are used improperly. For instance, the self-pacing is excellent for learning, but plays havoc with a classroom schedule. When instructors try to use a program under classroom conditions, they find some students finishing in the middle of the period and others not finished at the end of the allotted time. The fault is not in the programs, of course, but the problem does exist.

Another disadvantage is that, like teachers, not all programs are good programs. There are some criteria for judging programs, but even with these, bad ones still get into use. How can the instructors know whether a program is good or bad? Not by looking at it or thumbing through it. They can see what the objectives are. They can look at the criterion test to see if it tests what they want taught. They can see whether the program was given to a large enough sample, and who the sample was. But still, they may just have to try the program out on some of their own employees to see if they can meet the objectives when they finish it.

Another drawback is the lack of prepared programs in specific job-oriented areas. If the framus machine is peculiar to one business, there isn't likely to be a framus machine program on the open market.

Even with the disadvantages mentioned, and others that exist, the instructor may find ample use for programs in his or her teaching assignment.

PI AND ADVANCED ASSIGNMENTS

If instructors want the trainees to be at a certain level of learning when they show up the first day, they may send them an advance assignment. It may take several forms. "Read Chapters 6 and 7; study the material in this handbook; answer these questions and send them in ahead of time; be prepared to take a test on this material . . . " If a programed course is available, there is no surer way to make certain that the students will be at a specific level when they arrive than for them to do the program. If Boolean Algebra is a prerequisite, send them a programed text on Boolean Algebra, tell them to go through it and send in the test at the end when they have finished it. Those who complete the textbook should be at a specified level when they come in. The same would be true of any other advance assignment. Be sure to allow enough time to do the program. They aren't likely to come prepared if they got the program only a day or so before they left their job. The last-minute rush before leaving home isn't the best time to work on an advance assignment.

Portions of programs can be sent out in advance, providing the continuity isn't lost. Sending out the middle section of any program is hazardous, because most likely the program was designed to be used as a whole, not in parts. Sometimes the programs are written by chapters or subject matter that may allow them to be broken into smaller sub-programs. Also it may be possible to use a portion of the program, *starting at the beginning.* No continuity will be lost, and the student will not have missed key words or ideas. Notice, however, that the post-test obviously will not fit if the trainee takes only a portion of the program. The objectives will not apply, either, since objectives are written for those completing the *entire* program, not just part of it.

The criteria for the use of a program for advance assignment are 1. Is there a suitable program available? 2. Will the trainees have time (or be allowed the time) to work through the program? 3. Is there a need to bring them up to a certain entrance level before coming to class? If all these questions can be answered "yes," then there is no doubt that PI is the best solution.

PI AND NIGHTWORK ASSIGNMENTS

If it has been determined that after-hours study is desirable and appropriate, programed instruction is an excellent technique to use, providing a suitable program is available. Again there is the advantage of knowing each student will reach a *specific* objective, and all will be at the same level—on this subject—by the next morning.

The self-pacing aspect of programed learning makes it an excellent means of allowing the students to work at their own speed. If one student can finish in 45 minutes and another takes two hours, no one is the worse for the wear. The one who learns faster can go on to other things, while the slower one still gets the essential material.

There is a danger in giving a program without specifying how much the students should complete. "Work on this for about an hour," is poor instruction for a program! In an hour each student will have completed a different amount. A better instruction is "work to Frame 200 (or page 73)."

One decided advantage of using programed instruction for nightwork is the fact that other types of assignments often place the burden of teaching on the trainees themselves. "Read and understand Chapters 3 and 4" is too nebulous to guarantee uniform levels of learning for the next day. Since regular textbooks are designed mostly for classroom use, or as assistance to an instructor, they do not make good self-study material. They are particularly hard on the below-average students and may cause them to put in more time than is desirable because of their difficulty in digesting the text material. A programed text, however, is designed to take the student through the material one small step at a time. It is also designed to teach, not to be just an adjunct to a class activity.

PI AND CLASSWORK ASSIGNMENTS

The most difficult application of programed instruction comes with classroom use. Not because of a fault with programing, but because of the way the normal class is set up. Specific times are allotted for certain subjects and the teacher must abide by the schedule. Since programing is self-pacing, some students finish before others. The instructor, not wanting to disrupt routine, hesitates to allow those who have finished to leave the classroom. If other work is provided, they will get ahead of those still working on the program.

This dilemma arises because only one portion of the course is programed. If all of the instruction were in PI form, the problem could be solved by letting some *go home* early when they had completed all of the prescribed programs and perhaps taken a final test. When only an occasional program is used it may be difficult to fit it into the regular schedule. There are ways of doing it satisfactorily, however.

One solution is to schedule the program immediately before the lunch period or as the closing exercise of the day. This way, those that finish early go to lunch or leave for the day earlier than usual. They are not constrained in any way, and can be cautioned to leave quietly while the others complete their work.

Another answer to the problem is to assign *less* time than will be required for even the fastest student, then allow the class to complete the rest of the program as part of their after-hours assignment. This would apply if the work was scheduled before lunch or at the end of the day also, for the trainees need not miss lunch or stay too late; they can finish the program at night.

Short programs—ten or 15 minutes in duration—do not create quite as much of a problem since the time variations in completing them are not so great. If some students finish a few minutes ahead of others, they aren't likely to get too boisterous or fidgety. Such programs allow for a good change of pace from the regular classroom activity and save the instructor from having to teach a subject that can just as well "teach itself."

Unless a program must be completed at one sitting to be understood (which could indicate a bad program), *portions* of it can be broken down and used as subprograms or units during class. Segments covering only one or two units can be used, then the program can be put aside for a later session. The instructor can use these segments not just for a change of pace, but for a quick review or to bring the trainees up to date. When the instructor has reached a point where he wants the group to be able to describe the function of the plate in a vacuum tube, he gives a program segment on this subject. Since it will take only a few minutes to complete, the group will stay together reasonably well. The instructor will review his notes, and soon start his instruction again. He will *know what they know,* because he will be familiar with the program. He will not have to assume they know it as he might if they were merely reading a chapter in a regular textbook.

It is possible to have a whole course programed and still need to have the trainees brought to a central location. The use of laboratory equipment, or the need for seeing mock-ups, models, or actual items, may make it necessary to have the employees work at one classroom type of location. The classroom will have individual desk locations, preferably designed so the trainee can work with some degree of privacy. The instructor will be handy to answer questions, check out equipment, or clear up any misunderstanding of instructions. Such an arrangement as this must allow the employees to go back to their jobs when they complete all the requirements. This may be *one or more days* ahead of others. There should be an understanding of what is going on so no stigma will be attached to those who do not finish early. Mishandling of this important factor can destroy an otherwise excellent learning situation.

PI AND CONVENTIONAL INSTRUCTION

The idea of programing classroom discussions has already been covered. Here is a way instructors can make use of programed instruction techniques. They lead the trainees to frequent responses, orally if possible, and allow them to be reinforced while they get needed feedback. The method is effective with all kinds of trainees, and is easy to do once the instructors get the idea.

But there are other things about PI that can and should be carried over to the conventional classroom. A good program cannot be written until a careful "task analysis" has been made to see exactly what performance is required of the employee. With this analysis, objectives can be written to specify the level at which the students should be after completing *this particular pro-*

gram. What can the trainees say, what skills will they have, what problems can they solve, what questions can they answer, what conclusions should they be able to reach, what concepts will they have? Part or all of these must be answered *before* the program is written. Not only that, but some measurement is prescribed to test whether these objectives have been met—knowledge levels, performance or skill ratings, specific questions, or actions are spelled out ahead of time.

The obvious question is, "How often do instructors take these pains with their classroom activities?" How often are performance standards prescribed ahead of time? They *always* should be, but seldom are. If the instructor wrote out detailed objectives, he or she would be able to avoid going into a class to cover what might actually be unnecessary material.

There is another lesson we can learn from PI. Since we know that students both work and learn at different rates of speed, we can build in individual assignments to allow for this. We can even use the faster students to help the slower ones. When the faster ones finish, they may well take a small group of those having difficulty and help them along. Instead of ignoring the variation in required learning time, the instructor can use it or make it less significant. The instructor can break the whole group into smaller groups and let them work on their own for short periods. The better students will tend to aid the slower ones, and keep them caught up. The faster learners are not being punished because their speed is being *recognized and utilized.*

POOR PROGRAM VERSUS POOR TEACHING

One final thought on PI. When a program does not reach a stated objective, it is said to be a "bad" program. In other words, when students fail to learn from a program, *the program is at fault.* In fact, it is reprogramed or discarded. How many instructors would be willing to adopt the same standards? It is easy to criticize a program when employees do not learn, but too often when they fail to reach a proper performance level during a class exercise, it is they who are blamed, rather than the teacher. Instructors should take this as a personal challenge. "If the group doesn't learn, am I a 'bad program'?" It is difficult to "reprogram" a teacher. Conscientious teachers, however, realize their responsibility for learning in the classroom, and are not in the least frightened by the prospect of having the performance of their group checked when they are through instructing!

Exercises and Questions

1. Since programed instruction differs from classroom instruction in that it specifies the amount to be *learned* but leaves the *time* variable while in the classroom *time* is constant so that the amount of learning must vary, how can we possibly use programed instruction in the classroom? (Use good brainstorming techniques!)

2. How can programed instruction be used to supplement classroom learning?

3. It is possible to "program" a lecture so that students are led to respond from memory because *key words* have prompted the response. "In 1492 a man by the name of ? (pause for response) . . " "Since we find the employee has been consistently *late*, rather than have an appraisal interview, we need to have a ? (pause for response) . . . " In each case a prompt question has directed the response. Now break the class into subgroups and let each group pick a topic and discuss how it could be "programed" into a lecture. After about 15 minutes let each subgroup report its example.

4. Question 3 assures that the student already *knows* the subject (having read this lesson, studied nightwork, done an advanced assignment, etc.). But suppose new information is being given. How can this be programed? Break the class into subgroups and try to solve this problem by coming up with an example. [*Hint*: Let the students come up with *conclusions* to be drawn from the lecture.] The lecture provides the *background* information.

chapter 17
ADVANCE PLANNING

Two things will cause the best instructors to fail—*not knowing their subject,* and *failure to prepare properly for their teaching assignment.* Supervisors should be given the right to turn down an instructing job when they know they lack sufficient knowledge and/or experience to handle the material adequately. Equally important, they have a right to expect sufficient time to prepare, even when they are expert on the subject.

MATERIAL MUST BE ORGANIZED

The reason for organizing the subject matter is obvious. The material must be broken down into units small enough to fit time slots—weeks, days, periods between breaks and lunches, etc. The curriculum is examined to ensure continuity. The schedule should be designed so that instructors never have to start off a day by taking just a few minutes to finish the subject they were teaching on the previous day. A subject should be finished by the end of a given day or else enough material should be carried over to the following day to maintain continuity of thought. This may not always be possible, but it's a good goal to aim for —*before* the class starts. Such things should be ironed out during the *advance-planning period,* not at the last minute. Hence the need for adequate time and serious effort by instructors.

HOW MUCH TIME FOR EACH SUBJECT?

The question of how much time to allot to each subject is an everpresent problem which should be approached realistically.

Too often the amount of thought given to this critical point is surprisingly small. Many times, the schedule is made out *long before the objectives of the course are even established.* This means that the instructor has been allotted a certain amount of time to teach the trainees to do a certain thing—before that certain thing has been established.

Custom (tradition) is an undependable guide in determining the length of time required for employees to learn. Since it is customary to spend "a couple of hours on this subject," two hours are built into the schedule on the basis of tradition. Of course, if two hours have been established as just the right time to spend on a certain subject, then there is nothing wrong with following custom. However, if no one can say for sure that employees in the past have learned what was supposed to be learned in the two hours, better evidence than tradition is needed.

Another erroneous method of determining the time schedule is to start with a *total time* and work toward the smaller parts. Someone decides that a week is to be set aside for a specific course. It is also determined that a certain amount of material is to be "covered" during that week. The error here is in *trying to force a specific amount of material into a specific amount of time.* A week may be too long or too short for the specified course material.

There's nothing wrong with setting aside a week for training, but the material should then be tailored to fit the available time.

Now, how can the right amount of time be determined?

First, good objectives must be prepared, even for the smaller segments of the course. Once it is decided what the employees can't do and how much of what they can't do is to be taught to them in this course, time assignments can be made. How long will it take to get the trainees to the point where they are able to do what you want them to do? This becomes the criterion for setting time limits. The schedule should include *measurement time.* It isn't enough just to assume that the time alloted will provide the trainees with an adequate learning experience. Means an time should be allowed for testing, to see if the objectives have been met.

What happens if there isn't enough time to properly teach the subjects alloted to the course?

Several choices are available. One which is chosen too often is to try to teach all the subjects in the time allowed. *Such an approach invalidates the objectives.* The objectives state what the trainees should be able to do, provided enough time is given to the learning experience. When the time is shortened, the objectives also will fall short.

Another and equally hazardous solution to the lack of time is to "make more time" by cutting into lunch periods and breaks, and perhaps even extending each day's session a little longer. Worse yet is to have the students come back in the evening because there wasn't enough time to cover the material during the day's session. It is a mistake to assume that just because the time has been put in, the employees have learned. Time spent in class outside the normal class is seldom as productive as that spent in the regular class period, *unless the students have asked for more time because they want more help.*

If less time is available than is necessary to train on specified material, alert instructors will reselect their objectives, taking the shortage of time into account. Then they will select only the material which is necessary to reach the new objectives. In other words, they will admit that some of the objectives cannot be met, so they will take a realistic approach and aim for a new target. Someone else may later choose to change this and require that all the material be covered, but the instructors have met their responsibility by letting it be known that there isn't enough time allotted to the subject.

CLASSWORK OR NIGHTWORK?

At some time early in the advance-planning stage the instructor is going to have to decide just exactly what is to be learned during the scheduled class time and what is to be assigned to after-hours learning. It is easy to give homework without any real thought as to what it is supposed to accomplish. This type of busy-work most often defeats the very purpose of out-of-classroom study. The trainees soon realize there is little tie-in or purpose to the assignments, so they either do a careless job of the work or fail to do it at all.

Why give nightwork anyway?

There are several reasons, the first of which is to supplement class work. Time will not allow for all the practice and application necessary for developing a subject fully. By assigning out-of-class work, the trainees get a chance to "grow" in the subject. They take the theory or principles they have learned during the class and make the application to more job-oriented problems. By doing so, they not only get a better understanding of the theories and principles, but quickly see how they can apply these things back on the job.

Another purpose of nightwork is to reinforce the day's learning. A review of the material covered by the instructor will help solidify conclusions and concepts developed during the day. The problems in this case are of the same kind as presented during the day, perhaps with some new or different twists to stretch the thinking of the trainees. As they solve problems, reach conclusions, or do experiments on their own, the material becomes more meaningful. What was almost understood during the day becomes clearer because of the reinforcement of nightwork.

One important function of out-of-class study is to help the learners find out what they don't know. As the instructor explains various concepts and shows how facts and skills relate to each other, the students may feel fairly comfortable with the information. They were able to follow the work done by the instructor, and perhaps even do similar operations themselves. But after a few hours have elapsed and the problems differ slightly from those used in class, the students are less comfortable and more unsure of themselves. The nightwork allows them to check their understanding of the day's material.

Equally important, nightwork allows the instructors to check on learning, for the next day they have feedback in the form of the previous night's assignment. A few minutes spent at the beginning of the class period will give them some idea of yesterday's effectiveness. Glancing at papers or asking key questions, they acquire a feeling for how well they communicated the day before. It enables them to adjust or review as they feel necessary. *A caution, though*: Getting answers to one or two questions from one or two students *isn't satisfactory feedback*. As discussed earlier, this is an excellent way for instructors to be lulled into thinking everyone knows the answer, when in reality it tells them only that *one or two* students know the answer!

NIGHTWORK IS NOT EQUIVALENT TO CLASSWORK

In giving nightwork, it is a mistake to assume that the students, by reading pages in a textbook, can learn just as much just as well as they can in class. Unless the text is self-instructional, it will fall far short of providing the motivation and enthusiasm that should be present for good learning to take place. Also, students require perhaps even greater motivation after a day of class activity. They aren't likely to tear into an evening assignment after a tiring day in the classroom, especially if the class activity was made up of dull lectures. Also, they will be less likely to get excited about a long night assignment if the class is held on an eight-hour, work-day type of schedule. But uninformed instructors may fool themselves into thinking that they need only say, "Read pages 112 to 323 for tomorrow," to motivate the employees to *learn the material* on those pages. It is not likely to work that way!

So nightwork differs from classwork. If the classwork generated enthusiasm, if the schedule wasn't too long, and if the material was well prepared, the nightwork can serve one or several useful functions. But it will *not* replace the daywork, nor will it cover up poor classroom instruction for very long. Remember, too, that local conditions often set the standard on nightwork. Indeed, it may be that nightwork is not permitted because of bargaining argreements or overtime restrictions. But whatever the local conditions, the instructor should not be satisfied with "We've just never done it." or "We always give nightwork." *Either is a poor reason for determining the best learning situation.*

THE LEADER'S GUIDE

One of the main functions during the preplanning period is the preparation of some kind of "leader's guide." But what kind of guide is best? What kind of information, and how much, should it contain? Should it have extensive reference material or just a bare outline? These are all pertinent questions, but they may not be the responsibility of the instructor. A pattern or policy may already be set and instructors may have to make their material fit.

If the instructor has a choice, however, there are several things she should remember in making up a leader's guide. The instructor should simply ask herself, "What do I need when I'm up front teaching the class?" If she has resorted to note cards, it may be a waste of time to do elaborate work on a guide. On the other hand, if others will be teaching the same course at some future date, they may need an extensive guide for reference purposes. Primarily, though, the guide should show the instructor *where she is, what she should be doing, and the aids she should be using to do it.*

This means that the outline should be extensive enough to show each major item and as many smaller points as are necessary to refresh the instructor's memory. Supporting data to supplement the material being taught are helpful; they aid in answering the questions that may arise. References to manuals or other key material are useful in case the students desire additional information.

Time allotments should be included in the guide to remind the trainer not to spend time on trivial points that might better be spent on important material.

Reference to visual aids should be made at each point at which they are to be used. Slide numbers and even a few words of description will cue the instructor on what is coming and will make for a smoother presentation.

The guide does not guarantee a perfect job of instruction. It can easily become a crutch, just like extensive notes or a written lecture. Instructors should know their material so well that they need to make only occasional reference to the guide. Many successful teachers prefer to have the guide at the side of the room, and refer to it during break or at lunch time as a check against their progress. The trainees don't mind if the trainer stops to check a point, especially if they are convinced *he or she is doing it for their benefit.*

One good way of getting an overview of what's happening is to have our guide show not only what the teacher will be doing at any time during the instructing, but also what the *students* will be doing. This is a bit of a problem if we aren't sure what the students will be doing! For example, we might say that the teacher is going to be "lecturing for ten minutes." What do we put under the student activity? Do we say that the student will be listening? Are we sure? We can be sure of what the teacher is doing—we can watch and listen—but we can't watch and listen to a student listening. This may mean that we'll want to put together some guided note-taking sheets on the presentation we're making, so the students will have something to do. We may want them to answer some questions along the way and even draw some of their own conclusions.

We have to realize that instructor's manuals can get very complicated, but all we need is something to remind us what comes next, who's doing what and for how long, and what kind of visuals or handouts or exercises will be needed. We can make another one-page overview sheet that gives a breakdown of the day's or week's activity, in very simple form. The teacher's guide should be useful enough for anyone picking it up, being familiar with the location of materials and the course, to understand enough to describe what comes up next, and to a fair degree, conduct the course. That's a good measure of our course guides. Are they just for us, or are they for others who may someday take over for us? Is the guide such that it outlines key points, as well as the vital mechanics of operating the course?

CHECKING WITH OTHER INSTRUCTORS

Frequently, several supervisors may be called in to teach different parts of the same course. This means there is a chance of overlap or empty spots in the course. The *training director* has the responsibility for preventing this, but each instructor should strive to see that such overlap or omissions do not affect the learning in the class.

If instructors think a subject has been covered when it hasn't, they may be building on shaky or nonexistent foundations. Also, if they are unaware that a subject has alredy been covered, they may waste time (and bore the students) by dealing with it.

There are several things the instructors can do to prevent this.

They can check all the outlines for the entire course, looking for suspicious areas. They can discuss with the other instructors any subject material about which there may be a question. They can use feedback from their students, perhaps with some pretesting to see what the students know and don't know when they come into class.

Ideally, *all instructors should sit through the entire course,* thus guaranteeing their familiarity with what the other instructors are doing. But this preview of the course should be with live employees, not just a *dry run* with only instructors present. Too often these are reduced to critique sessions, or the instructor may say, "In an actual class, I would teach so and so," but not really do it. Courses change, too, and if the course is conducted several times, the last time may look quite different from the first. If time permits, instructors should sit in occasionally on the other instructors. This way they will have a feel for the content and perhaps the trainees will realize they are doing it for their benefit.

Each instructor should remember that every other instructor will teach differently and use various methods and approaches. Instructors most often force the students to adapt to them, rather than the other way around. Within limits, this is unavoidable. However, the instructor should realize that it takes some effort for the trainees to readjust each time instructors change. Since some teachers go faster than others, use different phraseology, expect more, etc., the students can be frustrated by too much change. It can have a negative effect on their performance.

Another problem is that all new instructors tend to start off as though the students were just as fresh as they are. They may be surprised to find the students are not as enthusiastic as they are, nor perhaps as interested in the new material as they expected them to be. Also the trainees may have been worn down (or worn out) by previous instructors. The rule to remember here is that *although the instructor may be new to the students, the students are not new to the course.*

CLASSROOM PREPARATION

The instructor may not have the prime responsibility for the classroom arrangements, especially where there is a training director. However, no good instructor would dare go into a class-room to teach without first familiarizing himself with all aspects of the room. Is there enough light? How are the lights controlled? How is the heat and air conditioning regulated? Are the acoustics satisfactory? Are the projectors controlled from the front or rear? Will they be ready to go or are they still in their packing cases? Will the students be facing each other or the front of the room? These and many other questions should be answered well ahead of time.

In addition to other visual aids, laboratory equipment may be used. It should be checked out well in advance, not only to make sure everything works, but to ensure that sufficient spare parts are available. Many a good demonstration has failed because a 15-cent fuse blew and there was no spare.

An important consideration in setting up laboratory experiments is "viewability." It is not rare to find thousands of dollars of equipment set up to demonstrate a most critical point, the result being registered on a small meter which even the instructor can barely see. The impact is lost because the trainees have to take the instructor's word for the results. If the class were broken into small work groups, the members of each group could see the results much better. A few hundred dollars added to the budget will provide a closed-circuit television arrangement with a camera mounted on a tripod and a large monitor which can easily be seen by all students. The camera will enlarge even the smallest dials and meters, making the results much more meaningful and allowing the students to participate by reading the information from the monitor.

Laboratory equipment often comes in modules which simulate actual conditions. It is most important that the trainees understand *just what is being simulated*. If they do not, obviously they may miss the whole message. A good description ahead of time, with frequent reminders, will help avoid this confusion.

As has already been stated, any kind of visual must be seen to be appreciated, and laboratory equipment is no exception. Preplanning should guarantee that the equipment, demonstrations, and results are easily visible to *all* the students (not just those in the front row). This means that the *instructor* should accept the responsibility for setting up equipment and/or class room arrangements to be sure the students can see

Whatever style of classroom is used—table and chairs facing the front, chairs only, "U" or "V" shapes—the instructor should be sure all trainees see and hear everything they need to see and hear. Straining a neck to see around a head gets tiring after a while, and it takes a lot of enthusiam on the part of the instructor to overcome a bad situation such as this. It is much better to see that the students have easy access to all that's going on. It may be necessary to limit the size of the class in order to get the best learning conditions. The argument that, "It is uneconomical to run small classes," can be overcome with the reply, "It is uneconomical to run *any* class under conditions that prevent the trainees from learning."

BACK-HOME INVOLVEMENT

We have to realize that many training programs fail not because of poor teaching in the classroom, but because of poor preparation back at the job location. We aren't talking about precourse assignments. We're talking about the relationship between the trainees and their bosses. If the supervision at home isn't involved in a meaningful way with the training effort, there is serious doubt that the training is going to amount to much. If the supervisor announces to the prospective student that there's a training course to be held at such-and-such a time and place and the employee is expected to be there—and there is no further word about the purpose of the course or the need for the training, the course is in jeopardy already. To make it worse, if the supervisor gives the idea that the course is probably a waste of time, *it probably will be.*

There are ways of involving this back-home supervision. We can be sure the objectives of the course are clearly stated in terms of job performance. We can let the supervisor know the kind of deficiencies we hope to overcome. We can send any communication to the supervisor, and ask that it be passed on to the students. We can ask for suggestions for additional training; we can send out questionnaires; we can put the supervisors on training committees or task forces; we can keep them informed about new courses. In other words, we can think of them as our clients who need to know what's going to be happening, rather than somebody who's in our way. We need their support. They deserve to know what they're sending people to our location for. If we can come up with money figures as to the amount of saving the training is producing, we ought to communicate that to the supervisors. If possible, we should even visit with some of them to get their viewpoints on how we're doing and what we can do to help them more.

ADDING PHILOSOPHY TO PREPLANNING

A major contributor to learning in the classroom is the teacher's attitude. Each instructor should develop a philosophy toward training that simply says "The students will learn *because* of me, not *in spite* of me." When the supervisors are in the classroom to teach, teaching becomes their *job.* Just as they are responsible for performance on the job, so are they responsible for performance in the classroom. The employees cannot shirk their responsibility as students any more than they can fail to do their work back on the job. But learning is not to be left entirely up to them. The company stands to gain or lose by their performance, and it is management's responsibility to see that the employees have all the opportunity and motivation to learn in the classroom. The supervisor—as a teacher—should be willing to carry a large share of the responsibility for seeing that the opportunity and motivation are present.

Exercises and Questions

1. What alternatives do instructors have when they discovei that they cannot meet the course objectives because not enough time has been allowed to teach the subject in the way that has been planned? What is the best solution to this problem?

2. Discuss the possible ways of determining how much time should be allotted to any given subject. Which of these methods are usually used (in your own situation)?

3. What is the relationship between behavioral (performance) objectives and the time allotted for subjects?

4. How often does "60 minutes to the hour, eight hours to the day, five days to the week" affect the amount of time allotted to certain subjects? Is this necessarily bad, since work schedules are based on these same time periods?

5. Should objectives be written before or after time assignments have been made? (Take a vote by show of hands, then discuss.)

chapter 18
EVALUATION OF TRAINING

This seems to be the place to say some things that are pretty obvious. The best training in the world is no good if it doesn't correct the trainee's deficiencies on the job. No amount of training will make an employee do a job better if the training is done poorly. So the training must not only be the right training for the right people at the right time, it must also be good training. And at the beginning of this book, we defined good training as that training that produced the kind of learning we wanted, regardless of how it was accomplished.

HOW GOOD IS OUR TRAINING?

Most of what has been said in this book so far has dealt with preparing to train and doing the training. We cannot stop there. We must be satisfied that the training we are doing is producing employees who can do what is expected of them on the job. Admittedly, if we have prepared a thorough task analysis, have written a good set of objectives based on this analysis, have prepared ourselves to get the necessary involvement in our teaching efforts, have been able to get feedback from the learners, and have used visual aids to help our audience to understand our presentation . . . if we've done all of these things, we should feel pretty confident that what we have done will produce the kind of results we want. But, even then, *we still have to be sure*. We can stop here and pat ourselves on the back or we can take one more look and see how our students are performing on the job.

The important thing to note here is that we cannot tell how good our training effort is just by looking at the students *in the classroom*. We can only pass judgment on the training when we see how they are using the training under the everyday conditions of the job. Even if we have been able to simulate the job very closely, we still have not been perfect at it, so we still must go back to the job and evaluate our training. We need to know how the employee performs when the boss is looking over his or her shoulder, or when the machines are making a lot of noise, or when the men are talking about last night's football show while the new man tries to do his job. That and only that is the final test of our effectiveness as instructors. And it's a test we must make, for unless our training is effective we could be lugging the whole program happily off the edge of a cliff.

HOW CAN WE TELL?

It goes without saying that we cannot follow up on every employee who comes through our training class. We cannot visit every job location and talk to every supervisor. We cannot spend the time doing these things—else there would be none left for doing more training. So how can we tell how good our training is?

One way is not to try to visit *all* locations or all supervisors; just some of them. It is possible to see *some* of the employees working at their job locations and to talk to *some* of the supervisors. Which ones? There are two choices here. Either see your former trainees on a random basis, or choose the "extremes" (the ones you thought were very good and very bad). The worst thing that can be done is to handpick the people surveyed. It is much better to draw names out of a hat than to pick employees you think will be able to "give you an intelligent evaluation of the training program." The latter approach usually means that you are stacking the deck in your favor. If the employees are going to be handpicked, it is much better to pick those you felt had a bad attitude or were not very responsive to the training, and then choose others who seemed to respond well to the things being taught. Then the ones in the middle can round out the number.

Supervisors should be consulted, too. The employee may think he or she is doing much better, but the supervisor is still the final judge of the employee's behavior. The supervisors should be picked in the same manner as discussed above. Be sure not to go to friends only. Match them with those who are less friendly toward the training program or training as a whole.

What do you look for in these cases? What do you ask the employees? What do you ask the supervisor? It is natural to ask, "how good was the training?" There's really nothing wrong with this question, but it doesn't go far enough. Suppose they say, "It was great!" What is your evaluation? Do you go home and say everybody loves us? "Great!" is very expressive, but it doesn't really give us enough to go on. Before we write anything down, we should ask another question or two. Perhaps the conversation should go like this:

"What's your estimation of the training?'

"It was great!"

"You really liked it, then?"

"Yes Sir, best training I ever had.'

"Why do you say that?"

"Well, everything was run smoothly, the instructors were interesting, the classrooms were well lighted . . ."

"Is that why you say the training was great?"

"Well, it helps me on the job."

"In what way?"

"I can just do my job a lot better, that's how."

"What can you do better?"

"Oh, lots of things!"

"Such as . . ."

"Such as, uh, well such as er, just lots of things."

"Can you give me an example?"

"Oh, sure. Take for example . . . well, there's always . . ."

"You can't think of anything right now?"

"No, not right now . . . but the training was great!"

So how good was the training? This conversation hasn't really told us much of anything, has it? Or maybe it has. Maybe it told us that the employee hadn't related her training to the job she was doing. It may have told us that the employee was doing *all right* on the job, or else she would have blamed her training for not having taught her properly. But we can't really be satisfied with any evaluation that doesn't give us some concrete examples of how the training is making the job go better. If the employee doesn't see that her behavior is changed for the better (or worse) as a result of the training, then the time spent teaching her is hard to justify.

But the employee isn't the only source of information. The supervisor has already been mentioned as a possible source of a good evaluation of the employee's training. The supervisor had to spare the person while the training was going on. The supervisor was expecting results from the training. He is responsible for the output of this person, so he will be looking for a change for the better. He will not be satisfied (anymore than we will) to hear that the "Training went smoothly." The supervisor has invested some of his production time in improving one of his people, so he has a right to expect something in return. For this reason, he should be a critical judge of how well the training has succeeded. We need to take advantage of this critical judgment.

How do we do it? We can use the questionnaire approach, just as with the employee. We can ask many of the same questions, except this time we ask what improvements the supervisor has seen rather than asking the employee what improvements she has seen in herself. Again, we should ask for specific examples instead of generalities. (Don't just ask: "Is the employee better able to do her job now than before she had the training?" We really want to know *how much* better she is and in what things she is better.) There are two approaches here that can be taken, one which has the supervisor name areas of improvement without any prompting, and another which gives him specific subject areas to comment on. The advantage of the first approach is to see just how much the supervisor will attribute to the training and how well informed he is on what was covered in the course. The disadvantage is that he may overlook something that was actually covered in the course, so you will fail to get the information about that area. The advantages and disadvantages of the second approach are just reversed from the first. Giving him specific areas to evaluate keeps you from finding out how much he knows about the training but makes sure all subjects are judged. The choice is really up to us. We have to decide which of these items are the most important and act accordingly.

What other questions do we ask? We need to find out a little more about the supervisor's *attitude* toward training in general as well as this specific training course. We will want to ask such bold questions as "Was the training your employee received worth the time spent away from the job?" We might go further: "Will you continue to send employees to this training program if the decision is left up to you?" Then we can begin to do some probing about which areas seem to be covered the best, which ones the least, which ones should be dropped, which ones should be added, etc.

Are these questionnaires valid? Yes, if the *population* is valid, that is, if the sample isn't weighted and if the training program was long enough and intensive enough to make a marked difference in the employee's performance. Questionnaires, whether to the supervisor or to the person receiving the training, give us realistic results within ranges, at least. We may have to summarize that 75% of the supervisors felt that there was "much improvement" in the employee, 12% felt that there was "some improvement," and 13% felt they could see "no improvement" at all. But that's pretty valuable information! If we word our questions in such a way that they can be summarized in this manner, we have a lot of very usable information. If the results are favorable, we have a strong selling point for continuing or increasing the training. Also, if the results are unfavorable, we should be alert enough to make the necessary changes or do away with the training. It's much better for changes in or deletion of courses to come from those doing the training than from those receiving it!

Questionnaires serve another valuable purpose. They build a better reputation for the people doing the training. They let people know that the instructors (or training directors) want to do a good job and are willing to go out and try to find out just how good a job they are doing. It also serves as a barometer to let the training staff be the first to get a "collective" wind of any dissatisfaction.

But questionnaires can't do the whole job of evaluation. Personal visits are extremely valuable. Visiting the employee on the job will produce some important feedback. They can *show* you what they have or haven't learned. They can *demonstrate* that what they learned will or won't work. Remember, it isn't necessary to visit all the people who have received training, just sample a few. Even talking to a few will be of valuable assistance to your efforts in reshaping the training program. Often trainers may just want to have some of their suspicions confirmed, so talking to several people who have been through the training course will help firm up their thinking. It's always safer to talk to the trainees after they have been back trying to do their work, though, because this is the only valid test of how good the training *really* is.

JOB SIMULATION

Another way of evaluating training is by means of a form of testing that simulates job conditions. This may be done on or near the work location. The trainer simply goes to the employee, takes her off the job, and then asks her to perform a simulated task that approximates the job she is normally assigned to do. This is best done several weeks after the training has been completed, so you can be sure that the employee has had time to adjust to working conditions and pressures. This kind of follow-up is valuable because it is a form of "controlled" experiment that can be repeated at different work locations and measured against the same exercise given immediately at the conclusion of the training. This test allows us to see how much of the training is transferred to the job and how much is forgotten or lost because of some job condition. We can now start to investigate why the employee could do the work at the training site and not at the work site. We may discover other training needs. We may find that there is something about the organization of the job that makes it difficult for the person to apply his or her training—no matter how good the training. We may find that the *supervisor* needs training because he either is interfering with the application of the learned skills or doesn't understand the job himself. Just training employees and pouring them back to the work site without finding out what is happening on the job is a pretty useless objective for a trainer.

Let's look at an example of how we might use the simulation technique in testing our training program. Suppose that the training has been for first-level supervisors. One of its objectives

is to achieve more leveling in the work group and worker participation in the setting of production goals. The end result aimed
for is greater commitment to the group goals, hence greater ded-
icatior of the employees to the organization as a whole. If the
training has been effective, there should be less turnover, less
absenteeism, less tardiness, less sickness, fewer grievances, etc.
Note that on every one of these items a group having gone
through training can be checked and measured against either itself before training or another group that hasn't had the training. But we can go even further. We can take these supervisors
off the job and put them through some simulation situations to
see whether they really do level more. We can see whether they
can develop a strong commitment to an individual, then solve a
group goal, which means subordinating their individual commit-
ments. There are situational techniques for doing just these
things and they can be carried right to the job site. A few people
off the job a few hours will give a large amount of information
and tell us just exactly how good our management training was.

CRITIQUE SHEETS

Most training programs end up using some kind of critique
sheet at the end of the course. They vary, but each is an effort
to try to see how well the course went. We can get some valuable information, and we can get some erroneous data. We have
to be careful in interpreting the information we get, because
even if it's all true, it may be incomplete. Perhaps the worst
thing we can do in an evaluation effort is to depend entirely
upon the students to tell us how good our *instructing* is. The fallacy of this can easily be seen when we consider that training is
a skill, and very few of the students will be skilled at either
learning or teaching. (Just think, none of them will have even
read this book!)

It's not unusual to see a number scale where the students are
asked to rate the course, or the instructor, or the material on a
scale of 1 to 5 (or 10, 20, 100). The best we can get from this is
that they liked it a lot or a little somewhere in between. The
difficulty is increased when we average these scores and come
up with an average of 8.21 for an instructor or a course. Since
we don't know what an "8" is, we certainly don't know what an

"8.21" is. But it becomes a comparison game, with each instructor being evaluated against the other, without this being intended, of course. We start thinking that an 8.21 instructor is better than a 7.96 one, but not as good as an 8.44. There is little that we can do to help the instructor who is making a score lower than another, but we can guess that there is some *showmanship* missing, rather than content or teaching skills, if the scores are not terribly bad.

There are questions we can ask that are helpful, of course. We can ask for specific information about intended performance. "What do you expect to do differently when you get home, as a result of this course?" makes a good measure of what the attitude of the students is. It avoids personality, and deals with behavior (though it is admittedly an opinion about a behavior). We can ask questions about the content by asking what they needed more of, and what they could have done without. When we look at the results, we may make a decision that they need more of something or less, or that we need to do a better selling job on the importance of the things they think they could do without. Questions like "How was the timing?" (too long, about right, too short) are probably going to be met with a balance of answers, an equal division between too long and too short with most answers in between.

There are no stock questions that can be asked, but there are some stock rules for designing the questions. The first, and probably the most important rule, is to decide what it is we want to know from the questions we are asking. Do we want to know if we have accomplished the learning objectives we set out to reach? If so, the question should be aimed at getting an answer to this.

The second rule is to remember that general questions get general answers, and only specific questions get specific answers. We can ask a general question about the time, the visuals, the food, or the teaching. If for example we ask, "How were the visual aids?" we may find out that the students had a problem with the visuals, but we won't find out which ones were not suitable to them. If 80% of the students think the course was too long, we still won't know what to cut out or what to spend less time on. The question we ask must at least have a subquestion that asks the students to give us specific areas that could be covered in less time.

The problem with all of this is that we've forgotten another cardinal rule: to remember that *students probably aren't very good judges of what is good teaching.* Just because they like or don't like somthing doesn't make it good or bad as a technique. If we spend our time asking questions about their performance and their objectives back on the job, we will get answers that are much more helpful to us. Let the students tell us about *their* jobs, their anticipated performances and problems, and their desire to apply what has been learned, rather than what they think about our teaching techniques or our fields of expertise.

OPERATING RESULTS

In the long run, our training evaluation is dependent upon what happens back on the job. No matter how well the students liked us, needed the information, and performed in class, and no matter how good their intentions are when they leave, the value of the training must be measured in terms of *the results they get from what they do on the job.* Even if we are able to change their behavior, cause them to do the job differently—the way we want it done, in other words—and there is still no impact on the operating results, then we will have a hard time justifying our training expense and effort. If we aren't able to send home trainees who give more service, make more customers happy, sell more goods, make better decisions (which have a favorable operational impact on the organization), then why do we need the training in the first place? In fact, our reason for training ought to be because the present performance of the employee is causing some sort of shortcoming in the operation of the business or service. Our measure of success ought to be in terms of the amount of this shortcoming that has been eliminated.

WHAT ARE WE MEASURING?

One problem we always have in trying to evaluate the training programs is that there are so many things that affect the outcome of the training effort. Many of these things are out of our control or even outside our knowledge. Some of them happen before the students show up, while they're there, or after they get back on the job. If we aren't careful, we will get things mixed together when we start to evaluate a program we've taught. We confuse measuring the students with measuring the teacher, the content, the course design, and the organizational environment back home. Instead of evaluating the students, we may be looking at the supervision of the people and the personal lives of the trainees, the needs analysis that got us into the training in the first place, the teacher's ability to follow the design, the students' attitudes in doing what the instructor has asked them to do, the influence one student has on another . . . and on and on and on.

Without exhausting the possibilities, but as a means of trying to show how many things affect the final outcome of learning, retention, and application, let's look at the following list two ways. First, let's ask ourselves which ones have an influence on the results of the training in our organization, then let's ask which of them do we now measure (or would like to measure). If it accomplishes nothing else, this will show us the relative position of what we do measure as compared to all of the things that affect the total training effort.

Influence?	(Prior to training)	Measure?
_____	Accuracy of needs analysis	_____
_____	Proper selection of students	_____
_____	Value of course (supervisor's perception)	_____
_____	Value of course (trainee's perception)	_____
_____	Discussion with trainee by supervisor	_____
_____	Length of time away from job	_____
_____	Advance notice to student	_____
_____	Perception of objectives (supervisor)	_____
_____	Perception of objectives (trainee)	_____
_____	Family situation of trainee	_____

Influence?	(Prior to training)	Measure?
_____	Job urgencies of trainee	_____
_____	Time and travel requirements	_____
	(During training)	
_____	Homogeneity of group	_____
_____	Rapport of students with students	_____
_____	Rapport of teacher with students	_____
_____	Degree of "belongingness" of students	_____
_____	Time available for course design	_____
_____	Time available for teacher training	_____
_____	Explanation of course objectives	_____
_____	Size of class	_____
_____	Length of training day	_____
_____	Physical facilities	_____
_____	Acoustics, lighting, temperature	_____
_____	Visibility of visuals, instructor, models	_____
_____	Self-confidence of students	_____
_____	Confidence in teacher by students	_____
_____	Course design	_____
_____	Audio-visual aids	_____
_____	Instructor's presentation skills	_____
_____	Degree of involvement/feedback	_____
_____	Students' learning ability	_____
_____	Peer pressure—other students	_____
_____	Instructor's knowledge of subject	_____
_____	Instructor's experience on the job	_____
_____	Furniture arrangement	_____
_____	Appropriateness of design to material	_____
_____	Instructor's classroom control	_____
_____	Adequacy of student materials	_____
_____	Frequency of breaks	_____
_____	Instructor's adherence to schedule	_____
_____	Instructor's adherence to design	_____

Influence?	(After the training)	Measure?
_____	Students' perception of amount learned	
		_____
_____	Students' commitment to application	_____
_____	Applicability of skills back on job	_____
_____	Opportunity to practice learned skills	
		_____
_____	Acceptance of skill by supervisor	_____
_____	Reinforcement of skill by supervisor	_____
_____	Acceptance of skill by peers	_____
_____	Follow-up discussions with supervisor	
		_____
_____	Follow-up training	_____

CONCLUSION

There are other techniques that can be used to evaluate the training which can be thought up by any enterprising trainer, but the suggestions above will do as starters. The important thing to remember is that we must spend the time and effort to see how effective the training is. No matter how well we think we are doing and no matter how many laurels we get from the students while they are at the training location, we still aren't a success until the job is being done better than it was before the training. And we must remember that we aren't looking for praise; we're looking for the truth so we can improve our training if it needs it, and keep it unchanged if it's all right. Any other reason is secondary.

Exercises and Questions

1. Questions for discussion: How good is the training now being done by the organization represented by the group? How do you know? Is there any concrete evidence or is the conclusion based on opinion?

2. How could the training be evaluated? What methods are now being used? Are the supervisors of the people trained involved in any evaluation of the training? Should they be?

3. Subgroup activity: Devise a questionnaire to be sent to tne students after they have been back on their jobs three months. Devise this questionnaire so that you'll find out how much they are using the material covered in the training session, how much they could *not* use of what they had studied, and what improvements they would suggest. Include other items that would be helpful to the trainer.

4. In subgroups, make up a questionnaire for the supervisors of the employees in Question 3, asking for the same information.

5. Finally, make a questionnaire for someone who studied this book three months ago. File it away in the "follow-up" file and get it out three months from now. This will be a measure of how successful you and the author have been in trying to find out about this challenging thing called "teaching."

chapter 19
HANDLING THE PROBLEM STUDENTS

In this chapter we shall list different kinds of students that seem to show up in the classroom and suggest some ways of dealing with them. Thankfully, all of these rarely show up at the same time, so we can have time to deal with the few that do. First though, let's notice that there are some basic assumptions we've made for those who read this list and take the advice given:

1. Most students come to learn and would prefer to learn than not to learn.

2. Most instructors are interested primarily in helping people learn, not in meeting their own ego needs.

3. The instructors want to protect the students, not to show them up or embarrass them.

4. Most instructors recognize that they cannot do a good job of instructing the class when there is a problem student who gets out of hand; in this case they take some kind of action.

5. In most cases it is much better to solve the problem that is causing the person to be a problem student than to send that student home or remove him or her from the classroom.

With these assumptions stated, let's see how we can deal with some of the problems that arise. We'll name the problem and then look at some possible solutions—solutions that have worked for others under similar circumstances. The solutions

aren't guaranteed to work, but more frequently than not they
have worked for most instructors who have tried them.

1. *Student doesn't want to be in the class.*

There are a lot of reasons why some students don't want
to be in the class, and the problem is often compounded
by the teacher not having a very easy way of removing
the students. Sending students home isn't a very good solution, even though some of them deserve to be sent
home. If the teachers are trying hard to help the students,
this makes it even more difficult to send them home. The
better approach may be to solve the problem if we can
justify the time it takes. So, how do we do it?

We may never know why the person doesn't want to
be in our course, and at some point we may not even care.
It's behavior we're looking at, and it's a change of behavior we're wanting. The goal is to get the student to change
behavior in the class. If the students are acting disinterested, we take one approach; if they're making a big case out
of being there and are keeping others from learning, that's
quite another approach.

For the disinterested students we try something like
calling on them for things we know they can do, even if
it's a question about their jobs, or about something that
has previously been discussed in class. We get these people involved in subgroup problems and appoint them to
speak for the group (so the group will supply the information for them in case they don't do the assignment in the
subgroup). If the students persist and say that they aren't
all that interested, we can still talk to them privately and
let them know that we have some rules and regulations by
which all students must abide. We can also let them know
that we are sorry we haven't made it more interesting for
them and ask what we can do to improve their interest.
This relieves them of the blame somewhat and may free
them to talk about their problems.

The person who is openly disrupting the class with bla-
tant remarks about not wanting to be there must be dealt
with more quickly and firmly. We still have the option of

accepting some of the blame by saying, "The organization expects me to meet certain objectives and that includes as many of the students as possible meeting these objectives. If there is someway I can help you meet them, I'd certainly like to try." The students must know that we are going to conduct the course, whether they are in it or not. But at the same time we don't want to get so "power hungry" that we nail the person to the wall and take a very autocratic stand. (We can always do that, so we try other approaches first.)

2. *Student is having difficulty keeping up.*
Many students who get to our classes will find it hard to make the grade, as far as meeting our objectives for them. It doesn't mean they shouldn't be there or that they have bad attitudes, and they may not even be a problem for us. But if they begin to be a problem in that they get discouraged and stop doing the work or begin to interfere with others, then we have to take some kind of action.

As in the previous case of the disinterested person, we must first let this person know that he or she is a proper part of the class, that we accept them, and that they have a right to learn like everyone else. If we see early that they're having problems, we can help these students by getting them involved early in the course. We put them with more experienced students or those with faster learning capabilities, but we avoid putting them with students who are well advanced and who learn more rapidly than anyone else in the class. These students won't be able to communicate with the slower students and may feel put upon if they have to slow down that much. It is good to assign the slower learner to a good student but not to the class whiz.

We must be sure the slower student doesn't get discouraged and give up, so we find ways of giving some positive reinforcement along the way. Whenever they say or do something correct—no matter how small the success —we comment briefly or refer to it before the class (for example, "As Joe said a moment ago . . ."). Another way to build confidence in such people is to mix them in sub-groups, let the subgroups come up with answers and then have one of the slower students serve as spokesperson for the reporting. This gives them confidence and gets them involved. They will also have to work a little harder to comprehend what they're reporting and to be able to answer questions about the report.

There is also the prospect of having some remedial work, and it's sometimes proper to do that. It may not be called "remedial" and may be open to all, but we should be sure that those who are having a tough time attend. It can be the last thing in the afternoon and can be announced, "There will be a session this afternoon covering today's problems, and those who had difficulty with the assignment—I'd recommend those who got less than 70% of the problems right the first time—come to the session. Of course, the session will be open to anyone who wants to come." If some of the better students come, they can be used to help explain the material. This will help them firm up any points they're weak on. The relaxed atmosphere of the assistance session will usually make it easier for people to learn better.

As far as remedial work is concerned, we can always offer to assist the students who need help, if they want it. We should avoid requiring them or begging them to learn or do outside study. If they are forced, they'll not learn all that well. Remember, we are talking about adults!

3. *Student is ahead of the others.*
The reverse problem of the slower student is the one who has more experience or is quicker at grasping things and hence gets ahead of the others. He or she may even begin to get bored and wonder why they're spending time in the class anyway. This is another case in which the solution isn't sending them home because they don't need to be in the class. (That may even cause their supervision to think they're bad students and cause some problems.) When we think about it, we realize it's really a good problem for the teachers to have. It means that we've always got some

body in the class who knows or can find the answer. It becomes a problem only when the person's attitude becomes one of dissatisfaction or even contempt.

There are several ways of keeping the fast students happy and working. First, we can depend upon them and let it be known we're doing that. We tell them we appreciate their experience and that we would like to call on it whenever possible. We can ask these people to supply additional insight into sticky problems or serve as the "field expert" when there's some doubt as to whether or not we really do those things that way on the job. We can give them some extra assignments—for interest and challenge, not punishment—and have reports the next day. We can say something like, "Here's something I think you'll find interesting. I just ran across it myself and doubt the class would be able to follow it completely. Let me know what you think about it." These kinds of things build the ego and offer challenge which those who are ahead of the others usually like. We've already mentioned pairing these people with those who are having difficulty, and we can even make a specific point of telling them we'd appreciate it if they'd spend some time with some of the people who lack their experience. (It's never good to tell one member of a class that somebody else isn't very smart.)

4. The "know-it-all" student.
Every teacher is aware of the hazard of having someone in the class who knows it all and has all the answers, who should be teaching, who sees nothing good about going over all this garbage, and who doubts the teacher has any credentials to teach the subject—and wants all the class to know these things! The world accepts the apt description of such a student as a "know-it-all". Without going into some of the psychological reasons for such behavior, we at least need to see that there are some do's and don't's in handling such people.

First, we need to go back to our original set of assumptions. Our job is to help the students, not to show them up or embarrass them. We also want to avoid satisfying our own egos. Occasionally, we'll hear an instructor come into the training office and exclaim with much obvious satisfaction, "Let me tell you how I stuck it to that guy who's been giving me so much trouble. I really nailed him to the wall right in front of everybody!" No doubt it's a true description of what happened, but it's probably not something to be proud of. The teachers who do this, and enjoy it, are meeting their own ego needs rather than the learning needs of their students. They may try to justify their behavior in terms of needing to do it to protect the other students—and they may have needed protecting—but there are other things to do to protect them that work just as well as, maybe better than, embarrassing or ridiculing one of their number.

We must understand that when we embarrass a student in front of the rest of the class, there is always a hazard that the class will resent it and side with the student. After all, we're attacking one of their own, and they may feel a need to protect that person, even if he or she has been causing them some problems. It is a matter of timing as to when they will side with the problem student and when they will turn on him or her. If we wait too long to deal with the problem, they will take things in their own hands. If so, they may become so brutal we'll have to step in and deal with them instead of the problem person. Ironically, instead of dealing with the problem person as we should have done earlier, we may wind up having to take sides with him or her.

So, what do we do? As much as possible, we try to let the problem students correct themselves. We show some tolerance, avoid getting into verbal exchanges with them, treat them as responsible people, and try to ignore their "know-it-all" attitude. We might even put them with another strong individual who has shown interest in learning the material.

If this doesn't solve the problem, we have the option of talking to the person in private, offering to do whatever we can to make the course more appealing. We make it clear that we understand and are sorry that some people don't always like what's being taught or the way it's being presented. We are open to suggestions. We also make it clear that the organization approves of what we're doing and expects the students to go through the material pretty much as presented. We don't say this in a threatening way; we just point out that the course or material isn't ours, but rather that it is the product of the organization's efforts to bring people up to the same standard. We can also make it clear that we have no objection to the person going home now, but that we aren't ready to certify that he or she has completed the material satisfactorily. We can even offer to call the person's supervisor and ask for permission to let the student come home early. None of this should be threatening; it should be matter-of-fact, because *it is a matter of fact* that we will let them go home. As we'll see later, we always have the right to take command of the class and let the students know what we will and won't tolerate.

5. *Student is eager, answers all the time, has right answers.*
How can such a student be a problem? With all that eagerness and all those right answers, surely we should be happy to have such a person in the class! What a blessing if we had a class full of such students! Ah ha, therein lies the problem; we don't have a class full of such people. When there is only one, that person does all the talking and usually spoils our attempts to get the other students to do some thinking on their own. They don't have to think or ponder to try to come up with an answer, and thereby improve their possibilities of retaining the information. They just wait it out and sure enough our prize student will come up with the right answer. There is no effort necessary by the rest of the students—no strain, no anxiety waiting for someone to think the problem through, no chance to probe or to talk to others about possible answers, no chance for the instructor to lead them into the right answer. There is no real chance for them to learn nearly as much as they could otherwise, because our star student is always right there with the answer. We ap-

preciate the eagerness, and certainly we're glad someone has studied and has the correct information to share with others. In fact, we may have encourged this person in the beginning by reinforcing him or her with thank-you's, and praise, and recognition of the right answers. So, what do we do now?

First of all, we don't want to punish such a student because he or she participated and had the right answers all the time. In fact, we should find ways of thanking and showing appreciation to this student. We just have to be careful that in doing so we don't compound the problem. Some simple ways of handling this have their roots in doing subgroup work. We put them into groups where others have responsibility for reporting (we may have to assign reporters); this way the eager ones can participate but not dominate. We can assign projects to specific people or problems to groups by interest, and have them report in turns with a different person reporting each time. (We aren't doing all of this just for this one problem student. Such action solves several problems and offers good participation techniques for everyone.)

Another idea is to call on specific people or specific tables for answers, avoiding calling on our good learner unless we really need a right answer. If the person answers anyway, we can point out that we want to hear from other people too. (This is said casually, not with force.) We can even have a rule that nobody answers more than once each five times, or that no one can answer a second time until someone else has answered once.

If all else fails, we can always talk to the person privately and point out that we appreciate his or her participation and don't want them to stop having the correct answer handy. We go on to point out that we want others to have a chance to answer (so we can see if they're getting the information), and we would like for this person to be our "answer book" as it were. We strike a bargain: "You be ready, and I'll know I've got someone who can give me a correct answer when I need it. Let's see how the others are thinking first, then if they are having trouble, you help me out. Okay?" It's a pretty well accepted fact that when we ask people to help us, they are flattered and will do whatever they can to help.

6. *Student is eager, answers all the time, has the wrong answers.*
This problem is much harder to deal with than the one we just talked about. We need to hear from this person occasionally, just for the feedback, but we can't have the person constantly giving wrong answers. We can't always be dealing with wrong answers when we're trying to let the students discover the things we're leading them into. The things we can do are similar to the others we've discussed.

First, we can stop encouraging these students to answer. We often forget that just by acknowledging that they've said anything, right or wrong, we are reinforcing the fact that they answered. So when we ask another question, they contribute an answer. As politely as possible, we ignore the answer or look another way at another student. We're in luck if the class has formed the habit of holding up hands when they want to answer or participate. That way as long as other hands are up, we just don't recognize these students.

Another solution is to go back to the subgroup, letting the group either help the person get more right answers, or do the answering instead. Remember, we're trying to do more than just keep the person from answering; we want the person who's been giving wrong answers to start giving some right ones. For every student who is answering incorrectly there are several who have wrong answers but just aren't speaking out. At least his or her one is letting us know about the wrong thinking processes. If we're good at it, we can use them as barometers of how people can get their thinking messed up. We might even ask them how they arrived at their answers and see if others have that same answer or thought process. Anytime we get feedback, it ought to make us happy, whether or not we like the feedback itself.

7. *The "show-off" who's dying for attention.*
Not every class has its clown, but once in awhile we find somebody who just never seems to get enough attention

and tries to get it at the expense of the rest of the class—
and at our teaching expense. This looks like another
chance for us really to nail someone, and the temptation to
do it is certainly there. No matter what we say or do, they
will find something cute or smart to say, distracting the
rest of the class (and perhaps us too) from their thought
processes. Whether or not they are getting the material,
they are keeping others from getting it; and we can't let
that go on. Even worse, they may be stealing our thunder!
Their jokes may be better than ours, and we may find
ourselves becoming the "straight man or woman" for their
humor. This is where we start to get in trouble; if our egos
start to suffer, we may want to strike back at the people
giving us competition. There are better ways of handling
this situation than figuring out ways of putting the people
down or in their places.

First, we must be sure they're really interfering with the
learning process—either their own or others in the class. It
may be that they are just naturally "fun" people and don't
mean anything by it. The class may understand this better
than we do, so a little careful thought might save us some
trouble. Next, we have to see if the person really wants to
show off, get attention, be the center of attraction, or if it
is a matter of covering up embarrassment from not knowing what's going on. Humor is sometimes a means of es-
cape from an unpleasant or insecure situation. Most likely
the people who are "showing off" are doing it for a combination of these reasons. They like attention from the
group, and they can get it more easily by being the extro-
vert than by being the one who always has the right answers. (*Right* answers are harder to come by than *smart*
ones!)

One of the quickest ways of finding out if the people
like this are looking for attention is to give them some!
But we should give it to them in a learning-oriented fashion rather than in a humorous way. Let them be the center
of things by being chairman or chairwoman of a task force
to accomplish some learning activities, make a report, or
do some research. If we constantly feed their ego in meaningful ways, we will make use of their "problem" rather

than letting it hinder us. (In other words, it's serving us and the students.) If, when we give them attention in constructive ways, they reject the work part of it and revel in the attention, we know that we must take more drastic steps. Here again, we have to avoid the urge to play "oneupsmanship" with them. It's easy for us to be funnier, cuter, or wittier than they are, but that just won't serve the proper needs. If there is ever a time when ridicule and sarcasm are tempting, this is it. By the same token, if there is ever a time when such reactions are inappropriate, this is also it.

When dealing with the person in an open way has not given us the success we want, we may finally have to approach the person privately and reveal our feelings about the situation. We don't say, "You're disrupting my class!", but rather, "I feel we're almost competing with each other, and it may be that this is interfering with the learning activity for all concerned. Is there some way I can make things more interesting or helpful for you?" It's not so much that the people we talk to will come up with good suggestions, but they will realize that we're serious about seeing that the class learns as much as possible and that we take our job seriously enough to deal with any prob lems that arise. It also tells them that as of right now we're giving them the benefit of the doubt. *Later on we may not!*

8. *The rambler—can't stay on the subject.*
There are those who have certain pet subjects, and no matter what the topic at hand, they end up getting around to "their" subject. There are also those who just like to talk about anything that comes to mind, with little regard to the time element or the assigned subject. The least little thing will set them off, causing them to ask questions like, "That reminds me of something that happened the other day. What do you do when . . . ", and away they go, completely off the subject. It's frustrating for the teacher and distracting and irritating to some of the students, and it may cause others to get interested in the unrelated subject.

Altogether, it makes it difficult for us to keep on a time schedule and give the students what we've promised them. Do we deal with these people, and if so, how?

This may be one of the few situations in which we actually deal with the problem right in the class. We don't embarrass or put down the student, but we let the person know that we have allotted specific times to specific learning activities and that there are some questions we don't have time to answer no matter how much interest there is from the class. We may have to say something like, "I know that's a vital subject to some of you, and it needs to be dealt with. However, the organization has made some promises to your bosses to see that you have an opportunity to meet these specific objectives, and it wouldn't be right to replace them with something else."

If it is obvious that there is enough interest to justify some time, we can test the commitment quickly by saying something like, "Okay, I think it's worth some time. How many would be willing to give some time of their own if we run over late tonight talking about this?" We don't have the right to throw away a design because one of the students would like to discuss something else. If it's only *one* person, we make the same offer: "Would you like to talk about this in the morning before the class starts?" When that person says something like, "Well, some of the others might be interested, too," we say, "Fine, anyone who wants to come and sit in on the discussion is certainly welcome!"

We have one other solution when someone tries to get us off the subject. We can plead *no preparation*. "That's interesting, but I'd have to spend some time studying that more before I'd feel comfortable discussing it. Can we both think about it, and you let me know some specific things you'd like answered? I'll be glad to put some time in on it, but if we do, I'd like to be able to set some objectives and satisfy them." All of these comments say about the same thing: if it's important enough to interfere with what we're doing here, let's do it right, let's *both* show our commitment by giving some time to it

9. *Employee with the negative "This'll never work" attitude.*
It is a rare class indeed that doesn't have someone who is
certain that the old way, the way they do it, or the way
they've learned before is the best way. "After all, I've been
around a long time, and I think what I'm doing is working
fine. That new idea comes from people who just don't
know how it is out there in the real world!" Or they may
say, "We tried that once before and it didn't work then.
What makes the organization think it'll work now?" Our
problem is more than just dealing with this negative case.
We have new people who look up to those who've been
around awhile, and these negative attitudes make it difficult for us to come across with much credibility. This is
the one problem student that can influence the class more
quickly and more seriously than most of the others we've
discussed. It must be dealt with, and yet the problem is
not just to overcome the negative influence. We have to
try to convince that person to go out and use the new
method. We don't want just the new employees doing it
"our way"; we especially want the older, experienced ones
doing it the proper way, since they continue their influence on others after they return to the job. So, how do we
handle the problem?

Let's go back to our original question: what's good for
the individual and what's good for the class as a whole?
There's no doubt we can win an argument on technique,
doing it our way, even if we have to say, "Sorry you don't
like it, but that's the way the organization wants it done."
That is effective but maybe not very efficient. It's unlikely
that this approach will build much commitment from the
older employees, and the younger ones may see it as too
heavy a threat. It is a form of "cop-out". Fortunately there
are better ways of dealing with this problem. One way
that is sometimes effective is in a subtle way to give the
dissenters enough rope and let them find out for themselves that changes in procedures, more modern technology, recent research, new policies, or things the competition
is doing, make sticking to the old ways of doing things a
good way to get a stretched neck! This takes some careful
handling because it can look like we're trying to prove the

employee wrong—which is exactly what we're doing, but we'd like it not to be so obvious!

Ideally, we can handle this in a way that leaves the negative employee feeling he or she has actually contributed to the new way of doing things and to selling the idea to the younger students. Obviously this isn't going to be easy, but it can be done. If we take this approach, we first have to be positive ourselves. We have to believe in the method or policy and come across enthusiastically.

Next, we should do our homework to find out just why the organization is going in this new direction. We need to know the advantages and disadvantages, the considerations that went into the decision, and the savings or profits to be gained by this new approach. It won't hurt to have backup information handy in case tnere is some question. Our goal isn't to ram something down somebody's throat or to overwhelm them with what may end up being "overkill." If we are certain of our facts and have the data to back it up, we can be much calmer and more matter-of-fact about it and can casually present the findings/proof as we need to. The worst possible thing that can happen is for us to end up on the defensive about the changes. After we've gotten ourselves "psyched up" over the subject, we're ready to deal with those who feel the changes won't work. When they object to something we're proposing, we show our surprise, make it clear that this is something the organization feels strongly about, express our appreciation for their interest, and then carefully pose some questions that will lead to some conclusions in favor of the new approach. Remember, our goal is to get commitment on their part, not to prove them wrong and embarrass them. If we ask them for their experiences or ask them what would happen if such and such is done (all these things leading to conclusions we want), gradually they'll begin to accept the new idea.

Finally, if nothing else works or we can't get approval from them, we must at least neutralize them. This is simply a process of making it clear to the rest of the class, and to them, that there aren't really any other choices and the matter isn't up for vote. Then leave it!

There are certainly other problems that students give us as teachers, but by now we can begin to see a few patterns developing. As we said in the beginning, our goal ought always to be to see that all the students learn, not just the ones who have a "good" attitude. For the most part, these are usually employees of our organization, and our job assignment is to help them learn how to do something they can't do when they come to us. To that extent we are running a sort of assembly line, and the end product of our "supervision" is a student able to meet the objectives we set. In every student able to do that, we have a usable product. In everyone who does not meet that objective, we have a reject. Just like a shift supervisor, we are measured by the number of usable products coming off the end of the line!

Exercises and Questions

1. Break the class into groups and assign them one or more of the problem students mentioned in this chapter. Give them about ten minutes to discuss it and then have them report additional ways of dealing with each problem.

2. During a practice teaching session, have two or three of the class members play the part of one of the problem students mentioned. Do not reveal who has the assigned role but announce that roles will be played. Do this several times and then discuss how each situation was handled. Offer suggestions as necessary from the whole group.

3. In a general discussion mode, develop a list of other kinds of student problems that arise and let each person write down what he or she would do with that problem. Go around and discuss the various approaches.

4. In this chapter it has been stated several times that we should try to avoid ridicule or sarcasm. Divide the group into two groups and debate the issue. After several minutes swap the pro and con roles and have them debate public rebuke or embarrassment. Afterwards discuss it in terms of the good of the students, the individuals, and the teacher.

EPILOGUE

If you have gotten this far, you should be no worse for the time and perhaps you may be a better instructor for the experience. For those who made it to this point, let me suggest that you use the book not as a rule, but as a guide. Not everything in it will work for you, but some of it will. At least be adventurous enough to try parts of it! Instructing is both fun and hard work. It is frustrating and rewarding. But don't be misled—you will not be a good instructor just from having read this or any other book. You will be a good instructor, or a better instructor, because you worked at it!

Good luck.

INDEX